BUSINESS COMMUNICATION

BUSINESS COMMUNICATION

Sue Smithson BA, MEd

and

Jan Whitehead BA, MA

Croner Publications Ltd
Croner House
London Road
Kingston upon Thames
Surrey KT2 6SR
Tel: 081-547 3333

First published 1987 by Financial Training Publications Ltd
Revised reprint 1990

Published by
Croner Publications Ltd,
Croner House,
London Road,
Kingston upon Thames,
Surrey KT2 6SR
Telephone: 081-547 3333

Printed in Great Britain by
Whitstable Litho Printers Ltd.

Contents

Preface

This book has been prepared to help all the young people entering financial and business careers; it aims to improve their communication skills both in relation to their colleagues and members of the general public.

Although its primary purpose is to satisfy the requirements of the Chartered Institute of Bankers' Preliminary Certificate, it is also relevant for those studying for the Association of Accounting Technicians examinations and all young people in the first stages of their careers. The authors hope that young employees in banks, building societies, insurance companies and other financial organisations may find it a valuable text in developing their communication skills. As it offers guidance in the use of the English language, it may be of particular assistance to those studying for qualifications from overseas.

It can be used as a textbook to support college-based full and part-time courses or can equally well be used as a self-study text. It is also helpful to those who wish to improve their practical communication skills at work; communication techniques can and should be developed throughout life.

The book covers many aspects of communication — relations with colleagues and customers, correct presentation of business documents, effective oral communication and the essential underlying skills of listening, analysing and summarising. It also looks to the future by providing updated information on new office technology.

Lecturers and tutors may find the activities and assignments give useful support, whether they choose to use the book as a textbook with full or part-time courses or as an open learning vehicle. A Tutor Guide is available on request from the publisher.

The material has been selected to introduce young employees in financial organisations to situations which they may experience in their daily work routine. It is hoped that it will both be helpful in gaining the qualifications they require and provide a practical bridge to work.

The authors would like to thank the Chartered Institute of Bankers for providing the specimen examination paper used in Supplement 2 and Mr Geoffrey Martindale, the Chief Examiner for the Preliminary Certificate, for the encouragement, advice and guidance on standards. The authors would also like to express their appreciation to Mr Stephen Hennessy, a former business and finance student, for the cartoons which enliven the text. Finally, we would like to thank the cross-section of students consulted who have studied for the first Bankers' Preliminary Certificate and have given their usual outspoken reactions to the material! We hope that every reader will find the book helpful in assisting their career and personal development.

Sue Smithson
Jan Whitehead

PART 1

Introduction to Communication at Work: Principles and Problems

1 Working with People

INTRODUCTION: THE IMPORTANCE OF COMMUNICATION IN A FINANCIAL CAREER

When you first decided on your present career, did you think that your day-to-day work would be mainly about finance — calculating, recording, processing? By now, you are probably aware that an important part of your job involves communication with other people; these may be other employees within your organisation at different levels and of course, the general public.

People often think that this is the easiest and possibly the most pleasant aspect of their job. In fact, it presents a great many problems and can result in frustration. Ineffective communication costs money — in time, lost business, delays and wrong decisions; it also has a considerable social cost — the atmosphere at work can suffer and unhappy relations at work often mean unproductive activity and poor motivation.

Because we begin to communicate at a very early age, we think it should 'come naturally'. In fact, it is a much more complex process than we believe. It is for this reason that in business training today, emphasis is placed on communication skills. So what do we mean by 'communication' — what is it, and why does it present difficulty?

THE COMMUNICATION PROCESS

It may help to begin with a simple diagram which represents what we believe happens in the communication process and then build up a picture of the problems which can occur at each stage.

You can see from this that effective communication *should be* a two-way process which achieves understanding and the required results. It is interactive and requires response and feedback if it is to be successful. Let's consider each stage in the diagram more carefully.

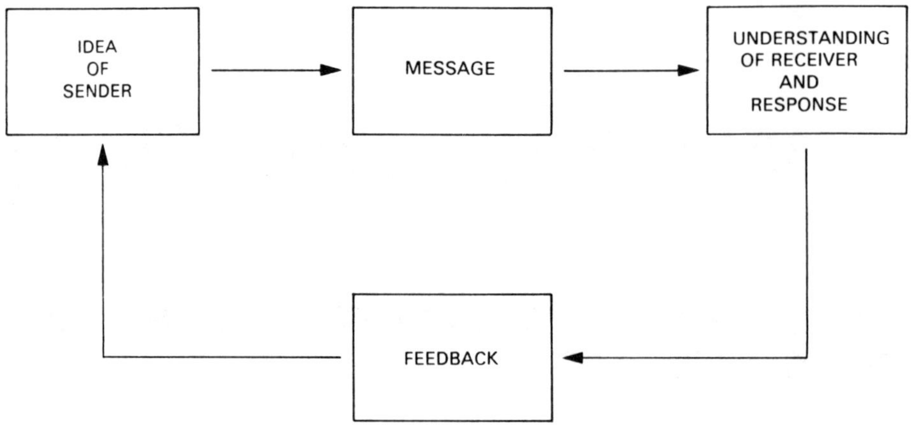

The communication process

Intention of Sender – Planning your Approach

There are a number of factors which you need to consider before you write or speak. The most obvious are:

- Why do you need to communicate?
- What are you trying to achieve?

You may want to inform or persuade; these are *not* the same objective and will require a different process.

ACTIVITY 1

Pause for Thought

We have identified that establishing the *purpose* of communication is one factor which any individual must consider. Can you identify any others?

Perhaps the quickest way of answering this is to list the other questions which you need to ask yourself. These are:

- *Who is (or are) the receiver(s)* in terms of such things as level of authority, degree of familiarity with the matter you are communicating, attitudes and age?

- *What method of communication* will be most appropriate in the light of all the questions you have asked so far?

- *How do you approach the person* or people in question; what tone, style and approach will be most effective in attaining your purpose?

You may also need to consider sometimes *where* and *when* people will be available and most receptive to what you have to communicate.

Only when you have answered these questions are you ready to formulate your message. Let's now consider an example which we will come back to later.

ACTIVITY 2

Pause for Thought: Example Situations

Consider the thought processes you should undertake *before* you communicate in two contrasting situations:

(a) A member of the public approaches your work station and asks to open a bank account.

(b) You want to change your holiday arrangements on the staff rota.

You should try to jot down the answers to the questions on pages 4 and 5 related to these situations before you read on.

The Message

Choosing the Most Effective Message Once you have undergone the initial thought process — planning your approach — you need to present your message in a form that people will understand; this is not always easy. There is also a second requirement, which is even more difficult. This is to ensure that your approach results in a *favourable response*.

There are several methods which you can use; you might select one, or a combination of the following:

Written letter, memo, telex, etc.;
Oral face-to-face, telephone, dictation;
Visual diagrams, graphs, VDU, video.

ACTIVITY 3

Pause for Thought

What is the difference between *understanding* and *responding*. Because you understand, do you necessarily respond in a favourable way? Consider the following question:

'Can you stay late tonight?'

Is this asking you whether you are *capable* of staying — or whether you are *willing* to do so? This question may be unwelcome to many people — how might it be put to enlist co-operation?

If you return to the question 'Can you stay late tonight?', at least this gave you the opportunity for discussion, feedback and persuasion to follow — much easier in an oral situation. Suppose instead you had received a written memo saying, 'All staff will stay late' — the meaning is clear but the response may be very unfavourable!

Individual methods of communication will be dealt with in more detail in succeeding chapters but a few comparisons at this stage might show how you can choose appropriately.

	Advantages	*Disadvantages*
Written	Permanent record which can be used for later reference	Production and delivery of message is slower than other methods
	Necessary for contracts and agreements	One-way method of communication, therefore feedback is delayed or non-existent. This can mean that misunderstandings cannot be sorted out immediately
	The recipient can take in the message at their own pace	
	Message may be more confidential	May be used to avoid facing up to a person
	More accurate for complex or technical information	

Oral	A more personal contact between sender and receiver Tone, phrasing and (in face-to-face) body language can help to convey the message Possible to secure faster feedback	Not very good for conveying complex or technical information There is no formal record The recipient can be more easily distracted by noise
Image	Can be used where it is difficult for people to read or hear because of environmental difficulties or disability Possible to convey information to mass audiences Can overcome language difficulties	No control over interpretation and feedback unless supported by spoken or written words Personal contact between sender and receiver not easy to establish May require additional skills to understand diagrams and graphs

These comparisons help you to choose logically. Unfortunately, it must be said that sometimes the organisation imposes rules or a 'house style' which may constrain your choices; as employees, there is little you can do to change this situation, except to strive to communicate better when you can and to improve matters in the future; all of us can become indoctrinated within our own organisations. It is always worth carrying out comparisons with other organisations — not necessarily in the same line of business — to see how successful other methods may be. Even the most conservative institutions have come a long way in recent years by carrying out this kind of activity — and on the whole the public is grateful for the improvement in direct and clear communications which has resulted.

Catching People's Attention An important aspect of delivering the message, however, in any of these forms is attracting people's attention before you begin the crucial part of your communication; after all, your message is only one of many thousand they will receive that day, and their minds may be focused on other matters. This is particularly true in an environment such as an open-plan office where many distracting messages are occurring by the minute. One of the advantages of face-to-face communication is that you can observe whether someone is concentrating or not; this is not so in written communication or even on the telephone where this kind of feedback is not available to you.

Some techniques which may help you to 'switch on' other people are:

- Making a purpose statement: 'I would like to talk to you about my appraisal report.'
- Asking a question about the matter in hand: 'Did you receive the memo I sent you yesterday about day release arrangements?'

In each case, the mention of the *subject* is valuable in focusing the attention of the person on the matter you wish to discuss. Cue questions are now built into software programs for this very purpose, and in written communication every letter or memo should begin with a subject heading.

ACTIVITY 4

Example Situations

To illustrate this let's go back to the two examples in Activity 2.

In each case, choose:

(a) what method(s) you would use to achieve understanding and a good response;

(b) what method you would use to focus attention on your message.

Whatever method you may choose, there are a few principles to observe:

1 You should *design your message with your receiver in mind*; in many organisations such as the Inland Revenue or the banks the language and/or forms may be familiar to the communicator — but not necessarily to the public.

You must deliver a message that people are capable of understanding.

2 Whoever the recipient may be and whatever method you may choose, *observe the six essential C's of effective communication*: it should be

Clear
Concise
Courteous
Constructive
Correct
Complete

You may think, of course, that you do all this already; remember, however, that this is your viewpoint which may *not* be shared by others; in fact, poor communication is one of the most frequently mentioned faults in the commercial world. Compare this with driving a car — we all think we are the best of drivers —

a view often not shared by other motorists, as their gestures make clear! How many times have you said something like 'Why didn't he do what I told him?' or 'Why doesn't she ever listen?' But did the fault lie with them entirely?

What other problems are there which create barriers to communication and militate against understanding or a good response?

Some Barriers to Effective Communication These tend to fall into two separate groups and can be listed briefly as follows:

(a) *Factors in the working environment*

- *Noise — open-plan offices are particularly prone to this.*
- *Organisation structure — the formal lines of authority may cause delay or distortion.*
- *Separation of working sites — between branches, offices.*

(b) *Personal factors*

- *Hostile attitudes.*
- *Individual perception.*
- *Contradictory body language.*
- *Poor timing — speaking as someone is leaving, etc.*
- *Poor approach — being patronising or aggressive.*

Most of these are self-explanatory; you can probably see the environmental factors every day. The personal factors, however, are rather more complex and are not always so obvious, so that often you run the risk of ignoring their impact.

Attitudes and Perception — a Hidden Problem One of the most important factors—and the most damaging—is that of hostile attitudes and perception. Anyone will interpret a message—or even another person or group—in the light of their current feelings and past experiences.

ACTIVITY 5

Pause for Thought

Sometimes, even our visual perception of the same event or image differs from someone else's. Look at the following two pictures. What do you see?

(a)

(b)

There are two common interpretations of each. It might help if you look at them with someone else to see if he/she sees something different.

The most common interpretations are shown in the suggested answer at the end of this chapter.

If visual perception can differ between people, their perception of other matters can vary even more. In the commercial world, the range of individuals in terms of their past experiences and their feelings will be extremely wide. The variety of response, therefore, will be enormous. It is essential to be aware of this if you are not to misunderstand differences which may result in hostility. Past experience is the outcome, among other things, of the times through which you have lived, as well as your education, family and upbringing. What we call the 'age barrier' is often no more than this and simply requires a little understanding. For example, some older managers may have what you regard as being too much concern for maintaining rules and traditions, extending to manners and appearance. In the more casual atmosphere of today, this may appear a little old-fashioned; but it is not necessarily wrong — only different. It requires understanding, and with it often comes respect for what, after all, is only a different set of values.

Body Language — Another Dimension in Communication Another major problem is what we have listed here as contradictory body language. Body language includes tone of voice, gesture, facial expression, posture. In face-to-face situations we depend heavily on body language to support and reinforce what is being said.

Problems arise when body language fails to complement or contradicts the message itself. You may have experienced this yourself as a member of the public and have been aggravated by it, so you will know it should be avoided. It is a subject to which we will give more attention in Chapter 2 on dealing with the public.

You need to be aware of the barriers to communication and consider how you can overcome them before you can promote the last stages in the communication process — the understanding and response of your receiver.

ACTIVITY 6

Pause for Thought

For example, when someone says 'Can I help you?', what do we expect in terms of their manner and appearance. Have a look at the picture.

You can probably imagine, too, the tone of voice which would accompany each of the above!

Achieving Understanding and Response

Reducing the Environmental Barriers

> **ACTIVITY 7**
>
> **Pause for Thought**
>
> Do any of the environmental barriers listed on page 10 exist in your own organisation? If so, what can *you* contribute to overcoming them?
>
> You might like to jot down some notes here before reading on.

You may think that you can do very little about these problems as they lie outside your immediate control. Sometimes, however, those who have been working in the same organisation for some time have become so familiar with the problems that they tend to 'live with them' rather than try to solve them. It might be helpful to discuss problems with those in authority — but only if you can make some constructive and positive suggestions. Even if you cannot eliminate the problem entirely, you may be able to minimise its effects in some quite simple but effective ways. If you personally find an open-plan office distracting, for example, you might suggest that space could be screened off in some way for work which requires concentration or confidentiality.

Improving the Personal Factors

Perception and attitudes Being aware of potential hostility and the possible reasons for it is half the battle; you can then prepare an approach which attempts to minimise this, taking into account the attitudes and perception of other people and building this into your method. If you want the support and co-operation of others, for example, you need to enlist this by approaching them in a manner acceptable to them, rather than confronting them with attitudes or a manner which they find unacceptable.

Body language Any individual in constant contact with the public, and others at work, needs to give positive thought to the ways in which body language might complement and support communication in an effective way. You might like to watch the next interview you see on television with this in mind! You will see that some are much better at using this constructively than others.

Developing a sense of timing There are several ways in which effective timing can achieve your purpose. For example, if you are in a meeting it is not a good idea to introduce important matters at the last minute as they will receive little attention; make sure they are included in the original agenda. Another positive approach is to ensure that the attention of your receiver is focused before your message begins and ends.

A further dimension of good timing is to gauge the right *emotional* moment for giving a particular message. For example, when someone is angry or upset about another matter is not the time to communicate an essential message.

Developing the Right Approach Often, working in an organisation puts you in a position which is in some way 'official' in relation to the general public. Unfortunately, this often results in your knowledge sounding patronising; this is bound to arouse resentment, especially in people older than yourself. A special effort needs to be made to overcome this problem and to ensure a friendly but courteous approach. Aggression, even when faced with it, is even more unacceptable and is to be avoided at all costs if you are to keep your dignity and, in the case of the general public, your organisation is to keep a client.

You may need to be particularly aware of the dangers here, too, when dealing with older colleagues, especially in other sections or departments.

Generally, people respond very well if you ask for the benefit of their experience — which, after all, is helpful to you — rather than assuming that you 'know it all'; it is here that the patronising attitude becomes very unacceptable and damages relationships at work.

Feedback

Every communication process should result in some indication that it has been received, understood and, if necessary, the required action carried out. This is often referred to as 'feedback'; in face-to-face situations a nod, or even a facial expression can indicate understanding; the eyes probably give the most significant signals here. Conversely a yawn or a glazed look tells its own tale! You need to be alert to all the feedback signals.

In written situations, such as a memo, it is important to state at the end the *action* you require to demonstrate that it has been received and understood — otherwise you have no way of knowing whether it is in the waste paper basket or not!

You have probably noticed in computer programs that once some information has been input you will be instructed what function to perform in order to receive feedback; this is because programmers have recognised that good communication involves inviting a response. To get the *right* response, they have also recognised the need to be 'user friendly' — a valuable lesson in any communication.

Example of a computer program 'user friendly' communication

```
*TYCOON* — QUEST — QUARTER 1

Do you want a practice round (Y/N) Y

OK, This becomes Quarter O, and the next

will be Quarter 1

Press any key to continue
```

Responding to Communication

Of course, sometimes (especially when you are new to the work organisation) you spend a great deal of time 'on the receiving end' of other people's communication processes — who may be successful or not. It is easy to criticise. What can you do to promote effective communication as a receiver — even if the message has not been clear in some way?

The Skill of Listening The first factor to identify is the need to regard listening as a skill to be developed, and not an automatic process. You will sometimes have heard the rather irritating phrase, 'I hear you' — often indicating disagreement! Perhaps, however, this summarises what usually happens; we hear, but do not really concentrate, thus missing a great deal of the message. Listening is a skill we often neglect.

There are many barriers to good listening; environmental noise, our own preoccupations, our attitudes to the communicator and his or her message are all involved. We live in a world where background noise — music in the supermarket, the radio in the car — is everywhere and it seriously detracts from our ability to develop listening skills; we *only hear*.

How then do we learn to listen? This is after all vital in the early stages of anyone's career if they are to progress.

Some simple techniques in face-to-face situations are:

- Focus your eyes and your full attention on the speaker.
- Concentrate on the *content* of what is being said without being distracted by physical appearance or mannerisms which may be annoying; consciously identify the main problems or facts.
- Take note of tone or emphasis to indicate what is important.

- Don't be too anxious to interrupt to show your own knowledge; however, demonstrate that you are paying attention by an 'mm' or 'I see' — this helps to convince the speaker you are still giving him/her your attention.

- Question and clarify when you don't understand — even though you may feel embarrassed it is better to appear a fool earlier than later when your mistakes become only too evident.

- If the situation involves instruction, or you are required to remember later what has been said, take brief notes — otherwise you will not remember; this also aids concentration.

- Try to ignore distractions around you and really concentrate on the matter in hand.

Signalling your Response

Communication is interactive; it isn't sufficient to take the message in — you need to *show* that you have taken it in and are responding to it. You often have to help someone to deliver their message effectively by providing different kinds of 'cues'. You know yourself that it is easier to tell a story or hold a conversation if the other person demonstrates that they are listening and interested by encouraging expressions and sounds. You must provide feedback if communication is to be successful — even if it signals disagreement.

ACTIVITY 8

Pause for Thought

One of the most common ways, for example, of demonstrating interest and that you are still listening without interrupting is to use the sound 'Mm'. This and other such sounds are technically known as 'phatic communication' or 'paralinguistics' — complicated words for such a small noise!

You might like to see how many ways you can use this sound to convey different feelings.

Again, listening to a discussion on radio/television will demonstrate how well or badly the interviewer/presenter uses this method to convey encouragement or the opposite.

All the principles discussed here hold good in other situations besides those which involve face-to-face communication, such as the telephone. Here the faceless voice makes listening even more difficult, and the principles need to be practised even more conscientiously and methodically.

COMMUNICATION SYSTEMS WITHIN THE ORGANISATION

So far we have examined the general communication process applicable in all situations. But when you enter a work organisation, you have to deal with this in the context of a formal framework; this is the communication *system* — that is, the lines of formal authority and relationships which constitute the organisational structure in which you work. This is often illustrated by an organisation chart — you may find a national representation in the annual report of your organisation or a local one on the noticeboard or in the employee handbook of your branch. Some organisations even have it displayed for the customers with photographs of the personnel concerned.

The lines which are drawn illustrate not only accountability, authority and delegation but also the formal communication channels.

ACTIVITY 9

Exercise

Look at the chart on page 19. It may be similar to that of your own organisation. Draw your own branch organisation structure and identify your own position within it. You might like to compare your chart with those of equivalent people in other organisations — particularly if you are studying as part of a group.

Vertical Communication

The lines of authority show vertical communication. This is used for communicating downwards, mainly dealing with the following matters:

- objectives
- policy
- general information
- instructions
- initiating change
- discipline
- advice
- consultation

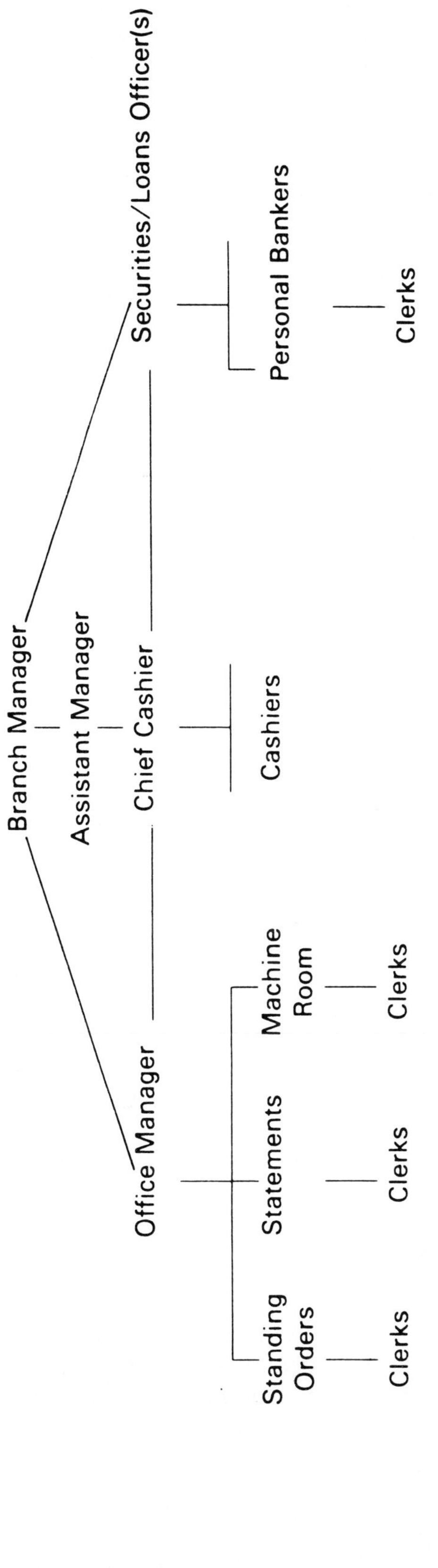

Example of an organisation chart of a branch

There is, of course, the feedback which we have mentioned before. Communication upwards is a necessary process if decisions are to be made well. Communication here might include:

- progress
- problems
- general or specific information
- reactions to change
- grievances
- consultation
- requests

Lateral Communication

Vertical communication is not the only direction involved. People also need to communicate laterally — across the departments and sections and between colleagues so that everyone can work towards achieving the objectives of the organisation. Matters communicated in this way usually include:

- information
- discussion
- dispute
- advice
- consultation
- requests

Direct Access — Emergency Measures

All this seems very logical and systematic. But we must not forget that communication is a *human* process; consequently, as in all matters relating to people, emergencies arise which have to bypass the normal channels if catastrophes or delays are to be avoided. All organisations establish bypass systems to suit their circumstances. You can probably identify some of these in your own organisation.

Some bypass systems are official — they are recognised and used by management as part of a policy of direct access when they feel this to be necessary. One typical example might be a staff representative having direct access to a senior manager at head office in the case of a collective complaint. You may be able to think of other examples in your own organisation.

Informal Systems

We now need to consider those bypass systems which we all know exist and which are *not* officially recognised — in common terminology 'the grapevine'. The grapevine grows for a number of reasons, and is used in a variety of ways — some good and some not so good!

Sometimes it allows official work to be carried out by methods which are more acceptable to employees than those laid down by the organisation. For example, let's suppose you need some information quickly; the formal system (that is, going to your superior) may be lengthy or you might want to demonstrate that you can find out for yourself and so you go to someone you know well in another section who has the information you need. This may result in quicker and more efficient work. (However, the information must be accurate!)

The converse of this is the confusion which the grapevine may cause when it is a source of rumour spreading dissatisfaction. For example, we have all listened to, and spread, bad news, which eventually proved to be untrue. Within an organisation, this can have disastrous results.

CONCLUSION — A REVIEW OF COMMUNICATION PROCESSES

You will be able to see from all this that communication, whether seen as a human process or against the background of a system, is not as simple as it seems. Within an organisation, it is often only too easy to accept the *systems*, and forget the *human process*. If the systems are at fault, this still results in frustration and resentment but it is frequently lost in the daily routine and becomes glossed over. Later problems are often not traced to their original source; this may be a failure in the human processes or the daily communication with colleagues and others.

Much more immediate — both for the individual and the organisation — are the problems that happen when communicating with the general public. Since it is on their goodwill that the organisation survives, while the basic principles of communication apply, the processes deserve special attention. In the next chapter we will look more closely at some of the practical problems of dealing with the public and at some actual situations in which you might find yourself.

ACTIVITY 10

Practical Exercise

Select one day at work, and during that day record your communications on the diary sheet on page 22. You should spend about 45 minutes on the whole activity.

Fill in the columns 1—5 as follows:

Column 1: enter a brief identification of the purpose of each of your communications, i.e. inform, persuade, report, instruct.

Column 2: give a brief identification of the content of the message.

Column 3: enter the individual or group to whom the communication was directed, e.g. colleague, superior.

Column 4: enter method used, e.g. letter, memo, telephone, face-to-face.

Column 5: enter whether choice of method was predetermined by the organisation or chosen by you.

After you have completed your entries under columns 1—5, look back over your entries and analyse them critically and then record in column 6 whether you think the method was appropriate to achieve the purpose of the communication.

Once you have completed your own communications diary, it is worth discussing your analysis with another member of your group to secure another perception of appropriate communication methods.

Communication Diary

1 Purpose	2 Content	3 Receiver/s	4 Method/s	5 Who chose method	6 Your comments

SUGGESTED ANSWER TO ACTIVITY 5

Picture (a) can be seen as an attractive young woman, or as an old witch; picture (b) can be seen as a duck or a rabbit. If you failed to see all these — keep trying! The illustrations on page 24 may help you.

ASSIGNMENT

Situation

You have now been at work within your present organisation for 13 months. You rather expected some kind of interview to review your progress and possibly

Old woman

Young woman

Clear pictures of an old and a young woman. Sources: Robert Leeper, 'A study of a neglected portion of the field of learning — the development of sensory organization', *Journal of Genetic Psychology*, March 1935, p.62

your salary after one year, but so far you have received no notification of this. You have been studying on an evening basis, and have had good results in your first year. You know the local college will have communicated this to your employers but so far no one has mentioned these to you on a formal basis (although your immediate superior has briefly said 'Well done').

You now feel slightly disconcerted and confused. Where should you go from here and how is your performance being assessed at work? You feel that you would like to discuss this with someone in authority, to find out what your immediate and long-term prospects might be. Before you can initiate this discussion, you know that you will have to answer some basic questions:

Problems

(a) Who would you approach about the possibility of such an interview within your organisation structure? Give your reasons.

(b) What checklists would you prepare for yourself to ensure that you had:

- (i) planned your *approach* to the person in question;
- (ii) chosen the right *method* of communication;
- (iii) given yourself the best chance of gaining the right *response* — an agreement to interview you?

(c) If such an interview were then granted, what steps would you take to prepare yourself to give the most appropriate initial impression?

PART 2

Communicating with the Public

2 Telephone and Face-to-Face Communication

There are several ways in which you communicate with the public, some of them more direct and personal than others. The most direct is obviously face-to-face across the counter or desk. Perhaps more usual, however, certainly at the early point in your career, is the telephone — an apparently easy communication method, which nevertheless is misused surprisingly often! These methods will be the topic for this chapter. The least personal forms are the letter and the telex message and these will be covered in a separate chapter. All these methods are subject to current and future change in terms of both techniques and cost-effectiveness owing to the increased use of information technology; the impact of this will be discussed briefly in Chapter 4.

THE IMPORTANCE OF GOOD PUBLIC RELATIONS

Whatever the method used, however, one principle remains paramount — that of establishing and maintaining good public relations on behalf of your organisation. The public will judge the credibility of your bank in terms of the service *you* provide and the impression you make on them, however junior your position. The public does not easily forgive poor service, discourtesy or an offhand attitude because of youth or inexperience. Likewise, they are not concerned with your work problems, or your personal ones for that matter — which you may see as a reason for lower standards occasionally. They have consistently high expectations of competence, efficiency and courtesy from those to whom they have entrusted their financial affairs.

Ironically, they will often display poor behaviour themselves; at the worst they may show aggression, bad temper, impatience or rudeness; more usually they may be inconsiderate of others, often indulging in taking up unnecessary time while a long queue forms behind them. There are other problems which you may have to face in dealing with the public.

ACTIVITY 1

Pause for Thought

Perhaps you have had experience of difficulties other than those mentioned above in dealing with the public either face-to-face or by phone. It might be useful to make a note of these now so that you can discuss them later with a tutor or colleagues.

Obviously, there are a number of other potential problems; one which you might have identified is that people often exhibit confusion or bewilderment when faced by procedures designed by financial institutions, or they are simply embarrassed by having to talk about their financial affairs, especially to younger people.

In any of these cases, it is your approach and manner which decide the tone and direction of the transaction and leave a lasting impression. Referring them to a senior employee can be the right thing to do on occasions, but the initial impression will be of you — it may decide whether they wait to talk to anyone else or not!

BASIC SKILLS — LISTENING AND SPEAKING

It is important to try consciously to develop greater expertise in two skills — listening and speaking effectively. Chapter 1 covered the basic skill of listening (see pages 16–17).

Speaking

The following points should be considered when you are speaking to other people in a face-to-face situation or on the telephone.

Your tone, delivery and diction are all important in creating the right impression and producing a favourable response. Some points to remember are:

(a) *Diction and delivery*: You need to speak clearly and audibly; if you are using the telephone or speaking to someone with a language difference it also helps to slow down. It is embarrassing for people to have to ask you to repeat what you have said and this can be avoided if you pronounce your words clearly.

If they do not understand the first time, try to avoid the temptation to merely repeat your words or to speak more loudly (which we all do at times). It is better to rephrase what you have said in a clearer or simpler way.

(b) *Tone*: You may remember a very well-known advertisement for a building society which concentrated on a young lady with a smile on her face and in her voice as being a 'welcoming' image for the society as a whole. It carries an important lesson — people respond better to someone who looks or sounds confident, cheerful and ready to help. Have another look at the cartoon on page 13 for example.

We have established that there are a number of problems in dealing with the public and that there is an overriding need to promote good public relations. Now let's look in more detail at the various situations in which you will be communicating with customers.

TELEPHONE

Frequently you are required to receive and answer queries, or even complaints, by telephone. Good telephone technique and a courteous manner can achieve a favourable response. Unfortunately, these are surprisingly rare, especially as a combination — it's no good being generally pleasant at great length but to little point — your telephone calls are scarcely going to be cost-effective! It is worth considering some basic principles which can help you to answer and make calls more competently.

Answering Telephone Calls

Doing this efficiently requires you to observe a number of points which can be listed as follows:

(a) *Familiarise yourself with your telephone system* and its facilities as part of your self-training when you enter the organisation. Examples of questions you will need to answer are:

- Is there a main switchboard which establishes the identity of the bank and then transfers the call to an extension or are you on a direct line?
- How do you transfer/re-route calls?
- Is there a teleconferencing facility (i.e. can you talk to more than one extension at once)?
- Is there a memory facility for storing telephone numbers?

(b) *Organise your work space* Have near the telephone the following items:

- An internal directory so that you can re-route/transfer calls immediately and correctly if necessary (many customers are not clear about the section which can answer their query).

MESSAGE FOR

M..

WHILE YOU WERE OUT

M..

OF..

TELEPHONE NO. ....

TELEPHONED		PLEASE RING	
CALLED TO SEE YOU		WILL CALL AGAIN	
WANTS TO SEE YOU		URGENT	

MESSAGE: ....

....

....

....

DATE.................................. TIME..............................

RECEIVED BY..

- A message pad and pencil/pen — a typical example of a telephone message pad is shown on page 30.

- Your diary or planner.

- Your personal computer/terminal (if you are required to input data immediately).

It is also a good idea to *file close at hand* the *information* which is most *frequently needed* to answer the most usual queries. You do not want to leave the caller in the situation of 'hanging on' for too long.

(c) *Answering the call*

- You can only establish a rapport with the caller with your voice. Try to make your *voice cheerful, courteous and audible.*

- *Establish a routine procedure* for answering calls. Normally the switchboard will have identified the organisation and transferred the call to the section asked for (or the one most likely to be able to answer the query). When you answer an extension, you need to:

  (i) give a greeting;
  (ii) announce your section and your name;
  (iii) find out the purpose of the customer's call.

Be careful, however, that your tone and approach promote good public relations. Don't, for example, open by saying, 'Hello, Sharp, Securities'. This is abrupt and sounds, at the same time, too informal and rather aggressive. It is also ambiguous. It sounds as though you work for Sharp Securities! Instead, 'Good morning, Nicholas Sharp speaking in the Securities department. How can I help you?' The impression is entirely different.

(d) *Obtaining information*

- *Clarify the reason* for the call — the customer may be uncertain, and unsure even of the bank's terminology concerning some queries. Some (tactful) information giving is helpful here.

- If the call is not something you can answer, re-route but remain helpful and informative as possible. Always state to whom you are re-routing and why.

- If the query is complex you will need to concentrate and demonstrate attention.

(e) *Recording information*

- Take notes — do not rely on memory.
- Check back on figures, times, dates, proper names — anything which you may have misheard. It is useful to check back 'one-five' for 15, for example — it is easily misheard for 50.
- A copy of the phonetic alphabet (see below) is useful for checking spelling.

Phonetic Alphabet (used internationally by British Telecom)

A	Alpha	J	Juliet	S	Sierra
B	Bravo	K	Kilo	T	Tango
C	Charlie	L	Lima	U	Uniform
D	Delta	M	Mike	V	Victor
E	Echo	N	November	W	Whisky
F	Foxtrot	O	Oscar	X	X Ray
G	Golf	P	Papa	Y	Yankee
H	Hotel	Q	Quebec	Z	Zulu
I	India	R	Romeo		

(f) *Relaying messages*

If you have to take a message for someone else, make sure that you have recorded it accurately and clearly and that the message is despatched to its correct destination *immediately*.

Making Telephone Calls

Extraordinarily, many people seem to think that there is no need to prepare *before* making a call — they simply pick up the receiver and speak! Perhaps you have been guilty of this in the past, probably at the expense of the telephone bill and other people's time!

ACTIVITY 2

Pause for Thought

What kind of preparation do you think you *should* make before picking up the telephone? You might like to make a quick checklist before reading on.

(a) *Preparation: establishing priorities* Clearly it is in the bank's interests if your calls are well planned, because this will also mean that they are efficient in achieving their objective, as well as short and concise. This will result in a cost-effective call.

It is likely that, in the course of any working day, you will have a number of calls to make. Obviously you should try to make these in the standard rate period after 1.00 p.m., although in some cases you may *have* to make a morning call in the peak rate period.

Sometimes your superior may have given insufficient thought to the timing — it's easy to say, 'phone Mr Brown' without thinking; so when you are asked to telephone, it may be worth checking whether you should do this immediately or whether it can be done in the afternoon.

In any case, the first step in organising your calls logically is to establish an order of priority so that urgent and important calls are carried out quickly, whereas routine calls can be made later.

It is a good idea to make a list in priority order before you plan further. The importance of each call may also determine other decisions, for example whether you may be willing to hold if this becomes necessary, or whether you would prefer to ring back. You could note this against the calls in your list, too.

(b) *Planning the call* The logical steps in planning a call methodically are as follows:

- Identify what you need to make the call so that it is all at hand and clearly visible. This may include the relevant file, letter or other documents.
- Identify the main points in the documentation to which you wish to refer. You will either need to highlight or underline in pencil or, if the document cannot be marked, to note these briefly.
- Plan the *order* of the message; it is easier for people to understand quickly if there is a logical order; you will need to note this in advance so that you are sure that nothing has been omitted and that you *do* follow the planned sequence even if you are interrupted, and/or have to answer an unforeseen query.
- If your call is to *obtain* information, have a list of the questions you wish to ask so that you can note the answers accurately and quickly during your call.
- When you are checking the number you wish to ring, make sure you note the extension number if there is one and the correct name of your contact so that if you have to go through a switchboard your call can

be transferred as quickly as possible. It is also a good idea to identify someone else to whom you *could* speak if your contact is unavailable.

(c) *Making the call* When making the call it is important to follow procedures which promote good public relations on behalf of your organisation and which maintain high standards of communication. These procedures can be listed as follows:

- The person who initially answers may *not* be the one to whom you wish to speak; often, for example, it will be a telephonist (it may even be an answering machine). In any case, you should give a greeting, announce your name, your organisation and, if relevant, your position and department; this is often known as the '*verbal handshake*' and is important in establishing good relationships. You should state clearly the name of the person to whom you wish to speak, and give their extension number if appropriate, and if you have one.

  Audibility, clarity of diction and courteousness of tone are of course crucial — in fact, the same principles apply as those discussed in answering calls.

  If your contact is unavailable, and you are asked if you wish to hold or speak to someone else, you should state clearly and quickly what action you wish to take, having noted this at the preparation stage.

- You can now follow your planned order, with the check-list of points, questions and documentation that you have prepared. Make notes against these as the call progresses, so that you have an accurate and precise written record to which you can refer afterwards; as with answering calls, double check proper names and numbers and concentrate on your listening skills.

- Concluding the call is more difficult than it appears! You may have had experience of other people at the end of a telephone who either lapse into silence, begin to digress or repeat themselves or put the phone down abruptly before agreeing what the next action or result of the call should be. To conclude a call successfully you should:

  (i) summarise briefly the main action points, and agree them;
  (ii) clarify who should carry these out and in what order they should be accomplished;
  (iii) end your call on a *positive* note, leaving the impression of an efficient but friendly organisation.

Finally, remember that the telephone can be a rather impersonal medium, and sometimes people can pick up a nuance which you do not intend, because your method of communication is limited — you have neither gesture nor expression to help you; therefore, your approach *has* to be established *only* by what you say and by your style and tone. For this reason, a great deal of thought needs to be given to the deceptively simple process of using the telephone.

Style and Tone There are three basic styles you may find yourself using on the phone. These three styles can be summarised as:

(a) submissive;
(b) aggressive;
(c) assertive.

The style you consciously adopt or unconsciously lapse into is likely to influence the way clients may respond to you and the ease with which you complete your business. In the case of a submissive or aggressive style you are likely to provoke a negative response. You should aim to adopt an assertive approach. The table below should help you to identify features that are characteristic of the three styles and to practise an assertive approach by your use of voice and words and even the way you sit at the telephone.

	Submissive Caller	*Aggressive Caller*	*Assertive Caller*
Voice	Is quiet and sometimes inaudible	Is loud	Is clear and audible
	Is hesitant	Is sharp and strident	Uses variety in tone
	Speaks too fast	Speaks fast	Uses a steady pace
	Has many pauses using 'ah', 'um', clearing throat	Emphasises words detrimental to client	Emphasises key words helpful to client
Opening words	Sorry to bother you I'm afraid	Yes? What do you want? I'm short of time but if you must	May I help you? How can I help you?
Frequently uses	Would you mind terribly if Unfortunately I wonder if I don't know	'I', 'I', 'I' I can't do that That won't work I've told you before That's *your* opinion	I believe that How about I need As I see it What would you prefer? Uses client's name

Personal appearance	Hunched over phone with tense muscles and breathing	Leaning forward or striding up and down	Sitting upright but relaxed so breathing easily
	Fiddling with papers, pen, hair, etc.	Drumming fingers or pen on desk	Notepad poised
	Tight-lipped, anxious expression	Angry	Smiling

If you recognise that you exhibit characteristics in column 1 or 2 try practising the voice and words from column 3 and try to be relaxed as you sit at the phone.

Handling Complaints on the Telephone

As we have already mentioned some telephone calls can be difficult to handle especially when clients may be complaining about you and/or your bank. Here are a few reminders about handling such calls:

DON'T

- lose your temper
- blame the customer
- blame other members of staff or the organisation
- pretend problems do not exist if they do
- make promises which cannot be kept
- hang up first

DO

- allow client time to let off steam
- take details of the client and the complaint
- apologise for specific inconvenience
- state clearly what action you are taking next
- keep the client informed of the progress you are making in dealing with the complaint

The situation is different, of course, when you conduct a face-to-face encounter; the whole process is more complex, and we will consider this in more detail next.

FACE-TO-FACE ENCOUNTERS WITH THE PUBLIC

In Chapter 1 we spent some time discussing the basic communication process, which includes such aspects as the importance of perception, attitudes and body language, in establishing contact; these aspects are brought into sharp relief when you experience face-to-face encounters with members of the public. In some ways, of course, these are easier than telephone transactions; but in other ways they can prove more demanding, particularly if the situation is an awkward one. An angry customer's voice, for example, is likely to be heard by many others, and you cannot hide behind a faceless telephone or retreat; you must negotiate then and there a satisfactory solution, often witnessed by other members of the public. Keeping calm on the telephone is much easier than keeping calm when confronted personally!

Of course, not all situations are this difficult. There are basically two ways in which you are likely to meet customers: in a situation where you are meeting them by appointment to discuss a given matter; and in a random encounter at the desk where you cannot anticipate the query/problem likely to be raised. The first is obviously easier to plan for than the second, and planning does, after all, give you some measure of control; some preparation can be undertaken for both forms of encounter.

Planning and Organisation

You can increase your confidence, and therefore likely success in dealing with clients, by taking time to become familiar with those aspects of the bank's business which are likely to be the subject of such enquiries and problems as may arise. These are likely to include:

- ▶ the type of services you offer
- ▶ the procedures and conditions relating to those services
- ▶ the benefits of your services compared with those offered by other banks, building societies or other similar financial institutions

Obviously, you cannot be an expert in some of the specialist services but you can know enough to answer initial queries and refer the customer to either the appropriate leaflet or the most suitable person in your branch to advise them further. Speed of response is often the first step to reassuring clients of the competence of the bank's personnel and the efficiency of its services.

If, of course, you are meeting by prior appointment, you should have organised all the relevant documentation and information in advance in order to conduct a quick, efficient, courteous and informative interview; if this preparation has taken place you are much more likely to be seen to be in control of the interview and to be offering a professional service. It is this impression which is likely to produce the most favourable response from the client.

However, knowledge of services alone is not enough in responding to all the needs of the public; the various aspects of your bank's business may have become familiar to you and a matter of routine; to each client, their financial transactions are a matter of personal and private concern in which other problems may play a part.

ACTIVITY 3

Pause for Thought

Consider the following situation: a lady approaches your counter and asks to open a bank account with a cheque for £6,000, drawn by her husband on a branch of your bank in Gibraltar. On being asked for personal details relating to address, occupation, present income, etc., she becomes reluctant to provide answers and is obviously distressed.

What would you do?

Preparing for the Human Situation

At this stage, you obviously do not know what her problems may be and do not have the training or experience to deal with them. This particular situation, in fact, involved problems of bereavement and repatriation and is only quoted to show you that it is good practice to prepare yourself for this and other difficult situations which you may envisage (or have experienced) which involve a sensitive response from you. Be aware of signs of stress in a client — such as hesitancy, incomplete or disjointed answers, facial expressions which convey uncertainty, resentment, fear, distress or anger. You do not have to be a psychiatrist to detect when someone is upset, for whatever reason, and you can give some advance thought to how you might deal with various situations. It is also a good idea to discuss methods of handling such situations with colleagues and superiors.

Of course, all customers are not as pleasant as they might be. It is now worth considering some basic rules in conducting any face-to-face encounter.

Encounter

There is a simple formula every encounter follows, which can be summarised as:

Welcome
Acquire information
Supply information
Part

- *Welcome* Remember how many ways there were of saying 'Can I help you?', which we discussed in Chapter 1. Make sure your welcome is friendly and helpful. Look up and greet the customer with a smile. Do not continue with your previous activity without at least looking up and acknowledging the client's presence. Alternatively, if your organisation has a signal to indicate 'position free', do not signal this before you are clear of the paperwork from the previous transaction and are ready to greet the new client.

- *Acquire information* If it is other than a routine enquiry/transaction, you may need to spend a little time on this. Explore what the client needs by asking open-ended questions (those usually preceded by what, when, where, how, who). If a decision is required from the client, indicate clearly what the choices are and ask for preferences. Again, remember your listening skills in encouraging the customer to give you the information that you need in order to be able to help him/her.

- *Supply information* We have already said that you may need to spell out the choices available to a client or you may need to explain a service. The rules of good communication apply — you should match your language and approach to the individual client. In other words use simple terms, be positive and accurate, concise and courteous. In pursuit of good public relations you should always describe services in terms of benefits.

- *Parting* Be positive! You should make sure that the nature of the transaction has been thoroughly understood and any action agreed before politely closing the conversation. This does not have to be effusive, such as the American expression, 'Have a nice day!', but do end the conversation with a cheerful smile and 'Goodbye'.

As you know, all wasps can have a nasty sting — in your case, the awkward customer.

HANDLING THE AWKWARD CUSTOMER

Types of Awkward Customer

These come in many shapes and sizes and you may encounter them on the telephone as well as in face-to-face encounters. Some typical examples are given below together with some initial ways of coping with them.

- *The over-talkative customer* This is the type of person who, however pleasant, holds up the queue. They are often elderly and/or lonely and will become upset or cross if you dismiss them too abruptly or try to hurry their transaction. Conversely, of course, the queue will get restive if the delay is too long. With this type of customer you will need constantly to lead him/her back to the business in hand politely but firmly and without rudely interrupting or showing boredom or impatience.

- *The angry customer* This type of customer expresses his/her annoyance over some incident/service loudly and at length. This is liable to damage your relationship with a number of clients who witness the incident. The customer

will have to be placated as quickly and efficiently as possible. It is not the time for you to indulge in righteous indignation or lose your cool. Apologise for the specific inconvenience only (don't grovel), take immediate action to put the matter right and tell the client what action you are taking.

- *The habitual objector* While some customers may become angry over a specific incident, there is another type who is generally unpleasant, surly and rude, no matter where they are or who they are with. Your problem is to ignore the rudeness and get on with the transaction as politely as with any other client and not to take his/her manner personally. After all, remember that this customer is like that to everyone!

- *The opinionated customer* This type knows better than you about the services your bank provides and insists on telling everyone else in sight. The wrong tactic with this customer is to challenge the accuracy of their information. You need to start by agreeing with his/her views but suggest further pieces of information for their consideration. Do not waste time on resentment of the implied insult in their approach.

- *The persistent questioner* This customer is suspicious of your reliability and authority and therefore questions everything you say and asks you to repeat information. He/she thinks it is possible to 'catch you out'. Be patient with this type of customer. Never pretend knowledge you do not have merely to get rid of him/her — you will be caught out. Stick to the knowledge you do have and find out if you don't know. Once the customer is reassured and convinced, he/she often promotes your reputation.

Dealing with Complaints

All customers will complain from time to time — about the organisation, services, personal manner, delays or mistakes which may have been made. The problem with complaints is that those who receive them are inclined to take them personally. We overreact and become defensive, if not aggressive; this pattern of behaviour is then likely to be repeated by the customer. The result is an extremely unprofitable confrontation where everyone becomes a loser.

People handling complaints need to think of them in a different way — they are a cry for help, a need to resolve a problem for someone who, after all, is spending time and money approaching us about it. Of course, we all make mistakes and it is how complaints are handled which distinguishes a really professional organisation from others — and therefore attracts more custom. There are quite specific stages to handling a complaint:

(1) You need to *listen to acquire the exact details* of what has gone wrong. Getting the facts right is critical if you want to calm the person down and give them the impression that you are ready to try to solve their problem.

(2) *Apologise for the personal inconvenience* caused but do not admit, at this stage, that the blame is entirely that of your organisation as this may be an admission of legal liability. You need to remember, however, that many customers dislike complaining and therefore their reaction to having to do so is to appear unnaturally aggressive or emotional, so you need to sympathise with the fact that the customer has had to complain. This will enable you to appear responsive to the problem.

(3) The customer is not interested in listening to excuses so don't waste your time or his/hers by giving them. Above all, do not blame another person within your organisation or any of its policies or procedures. If there has been a specific fault, it is enough to apologise and then *get on with putting it right.* To dwell on the past is unconstructive. You need to be positive in your approach and be seen to be making steps towards a solution.

(4) *Agree a course of action* with the customer that is satisfactory to both parties. If you cannot immediately solve the problem yourself, identify clearly what steps you will be taking to enable the matter to be resolved. The course of action needs to be agreed and to include not just what will happen but also when and by whom it will be carried out.

(5) A final, but very important point is that you will need to *check that the agreed action has taken place*, otherwise you will have an even angrier customer on your hands and one who might well want to remove his/her business permanently from your bank.

CONCLUSION — BENEFITS OF SUCCESSFUL COMMUNICATION WITH CUSTOMERS

These are twofold. It makes your job more satisfying to know that you can help to solve customers' problems and retain their goodwill towards you personally and towards the bank in general. The customers themselves are satisfied too because they view the services of the bank, which they have chosen, as being competent and professional. It justifies their choice of bank and gives them added confidence that their financial affairs are being handled in an efficient and caring way. They are therefore likely to come back to you with further business and to recommend your organisation to others. This is what promoting good public relations really means.

Of course, this is true not only of the oral communications which we have described in this chapter but also of all written communications which go out from the bank. These will be discussed in the next chapter.

SUGGESTED ANSWER TO ACTIVITY 3

You could persist in questioning the customer at the counter but the danger here is that she will become increasingly distressed in front of a queue of people who are not likely to be impressed either with the delay or with the distress being caused to a fellow customer. The need here is for an interview with a more experienced person in a more confidential atmosphere. This is the option you should give to this customer.

ASSIGNMENTS

1 A Telephone Message

You have received a telephone message which you need to relay to another member of staff who is out to lunch. Today is 9 April and it is 12.30 p.m. The transcript of the call is as follows:

Caller Good morning. Can I speak to the person in charge of standing orders please?

You I'm sorry, Miss Caudwell, who deals with standing orders, is out at lunch at the moment but if you'd like to leave the details perhaps I can help you by passing on a message.

Caller Well, perhaps that will be all right. Its the standing order for my mortgage which has just been decreased because of a lower interest rate.

You Could you give me one or two details please? First of all, can I have your name and account number?

Caller This is Mr Vito Corialli. (You interrupt)

You Could you spell that please? (Customer spells name) and your account number?

Caller 0908303

You To whom is the standing order made out and on what day does it go out?

Caller The Crowthorne Building Society. I think its the first of the month but I'm not certain of the day or the standing order number as I don't have my bank statement here.

You That's fine, sir, we can check that. What is the present amount?

Caller £330 per month and its now gone down to £310 per month.

You (Checking the figures and other details back with the customer) Very well, I'll get Miss Caudwell to make that alteration and to call back and confirm this with you.

Caller Thanks. I'll be on 0232 775870 extension 213 until 5.00 p.m.

You Thank you, Mr Corialli, I'll pass that message on to Miss Caudwell, to ring you on 0232 775870 extension 213 before 5.00 p.m.

Task

Write an appropriate message for Miss Caudwell on a telephone message pad used in your own organisation or draw up a form similar to the one shown on page 30 and use this.

2 An Awkward Customer

A customer approaches your cash desk with a cheque book for another branch and a 'gold' credit card which guarantees up to £250 withdrawal. He asks to withdraw £1,200, saying that he has an arrangement with his bank to withdraw up to £10,000 at any one time. He insists that he was given written information confirming this. When you state you will have to make a brief phone call to confirm this, he shows signs of becoming very irate; he insists loudly that he has a special arrangement and implies that you do not know enough about banking procedures to deal with his case. The queue behind him is growing embarrassed and restless.

How would you handle this situation?

3 Visual and Written Communication

Just as the oral encounter between people can affect the public image of an organisation for better or worse, the visual and written communications which are seen by clients can either promote or damage the bank's reputation. Again, they are seen as representing the degree of competence and care shown by the organisation towards its customers. It is therefore crucial that these achieve a professional level of design, composition and style as well as the most appropriate approach, language and tone. This is equally true of displays, brochures, notices, forms and letters, which are the most usual methods of visual and written communication between the bank and its clientele. Let's consider visual communication first since this is the most immediate method.

VISUAL COMMUNICATION

All banks spend a considerable amount of money promoting and advertising their services through the mass media and even through sponsorship of events or endowment of educational institutions. They rely heavily on visual material for their impact. However, the use of visual communication begins at the point at which customers first enter the bank.

Potential customers are struck by a number of visual images which have been carefully designed by the bank's marketing and public relations personnel to promote an awareness of the bank's identity and to encourage them to use its many services. For example, every bank has a logo and an image which is displayed outside, on its notepaper and in its brochures, e.g. the griffin, the black horse. We are sure you can think of others.

Brochures

In addition, much thought is given to the design and layout of the various brochures describing the bank's services which the client will immediately come across in the foyer of the bank.

Of course you are not involved in choosing the logo or designing the brochure but you do need to be aware that visual display has an immediate impact and can be more effective in communicating the bank's activities than written explanation alone.

The development of desk top publishing packages for computers has enabled many organisations to decide whether to design their own brochures, leaflets and forms. The use of such packages combined with a good laser printer enables documents involving text, photographs, graphs and charts to be designed internally.

ACTIVITY 1

Exercise

Take a critical look at the brochures on display in the foyer of your bank. How much interest do the cover designs arouse and how far are the images used appropriate to what is inside?

Look, too, at the layout of the information inside. Is it clearly headed and are there headings to guide the reader through the information? Does it contain any diagrams or pictures? If so, do these help to simplify the information or maintain the interest of the reader?

What would be your suggestions for improvements to the visual display of the information?

You might like to look at competitors' brochures as well. It is always interesting to make comparisons.

Graphics

Another document which a client might pick up in the bank is the annual report or the bank's review. These often adopt visual methods of communicating financial or statistical information to the public because they are considered simpler to understand and they make an immediate impression. Such methods might include pie charts, bar charts or line graphs — these are easier to understand at a glance than long tables of statistics (see examples on pages 47 and 48).

The production of charts and graphs has been greatly simplified by computers. Many graphics packages will now enable you to produce:

- *tables* — for columns of figures
- *pie charts* simple or exploded — to show parts of a whole
- *line graphs* — to display joined points showing sizes, quantities, volumes, etc. plotted against horizontal and vertical scales
- *bar charts* — columns of data set against one another for comparison
- *maps or contour diagrams* — for geographical features

- *symbol charts (pictograms)* — symbols (often graded in size) used to show comparative volumes or sizes to make statistics more interesting.

High resolution monitors allow good colour display of graphics. Financial organisations can use such packages to help in the production of annual reports, promotional leaflets, internal financial, marketing and personnel information, training material.

Staff Image

Many banks also concentrate on promoting their staff image to the public by using visual methods. Some banks have photographs of the most important members of the staff with their job titles on display for immediate recognition. Some also request standard dress in the bank's colours. Even printed T-shirts have been used to promote, for instance, a Saturday service. Generally banks display the names of their staff at their contact point with the public. This is all aimed at making the service simultaneously represent the bank's image and establish a personal contact with the public.

Pie chart

Office activities within a bank: clerical level

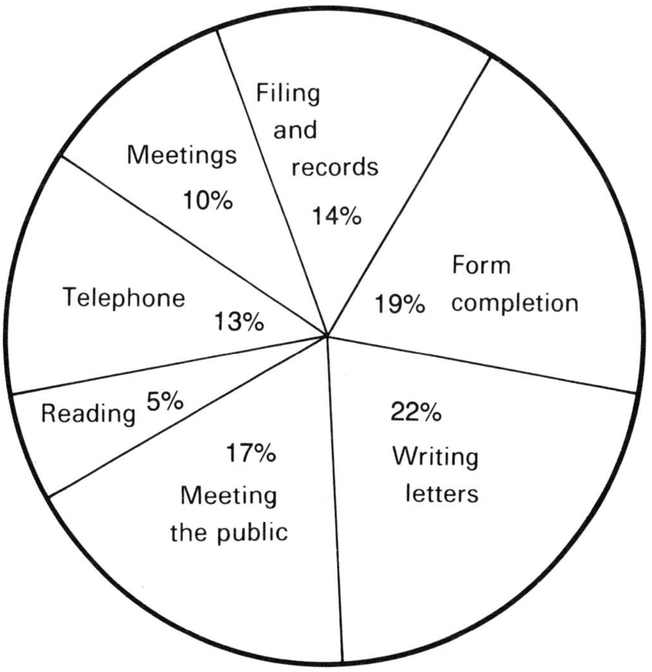

Line graph

Chartered Institute of Bankers membership

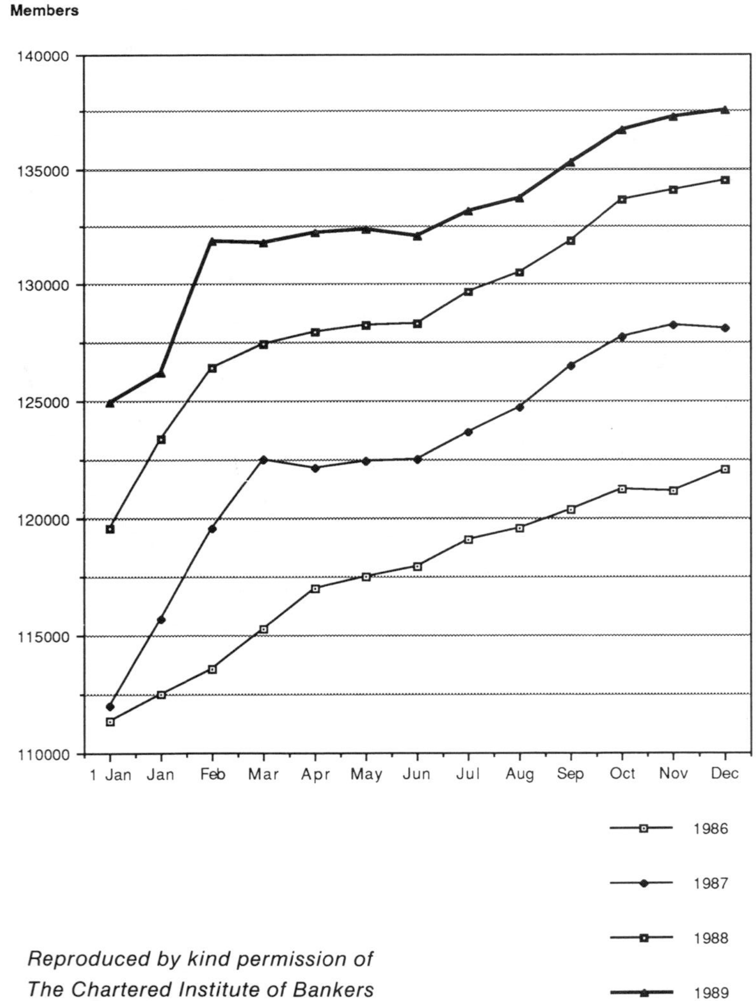

Reproduced by kind permission of The Chartered Institute of Bankers

Bar chart

New issue activity and stock market prices 1986

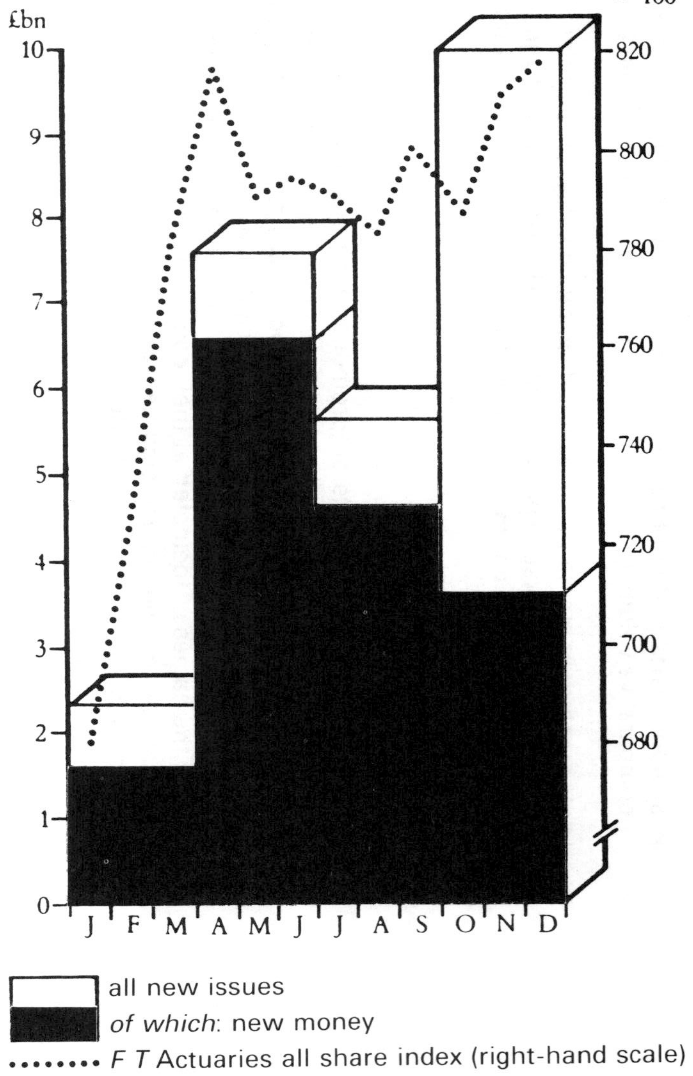

When you deal with the general public you need to be aware of the ways in which visual communication can help you to explain procedures to them more easily. It is often easier to show someone how to fill in a cheque or paying-in slip if they are opening a bank account for the first time than merely to explain it in words. Sometimes you may have foreign clients where your drawing ability combined with facial expressions and gestures may be vital! Later on in your career you may have to discuss financial matters with personal or business clients and an ability to present information in graphic form may be extremely helpful.

You are a representative of the bank and the visual impression you create will inevitably affect the client's judgement of your organisation — so of course will your manner and your ability to help with the various forms and written communications involved in the bank's business. Perhaps the most common of these is the business form.

FORMS

If a bank, or other financial institution, is to conduct its affairs in a reliable, efficient and appropriate manner it must rely on both its employees and its clients being able to complete business forms to provide accurate and complete information. Forms are the lifeblood of an organisation, just as much as letters, memoranda and reports. They afford a means of providing essential information in a concise way and logical order so that information can be processed quickly and decisions made.

Types of Business Form

ACTIVITY 2

Pause for Thought

Think about the types of form that are processed in your own organisation. What purpose do they serve? Who completes them? How easy are they to complete/process?

Forms come in many shapes and sizes and fulfil a range of purposes (in addition to the basic purpose of providing information in a concise format). They range from a simple message pad designed to help you record telephone and other messages in a logical order, to complex application forms for securing loans. Some are designed to enable the internal processing of bank business to be accomplished more simply and easily, such as forms for recording over the counter money transactions or to record progress. Others are designed for use by clients in applying for services or authorising their financial transactions.

These are very different areas of use and the design of the forms needs to reflect this. For instance, if you are a bank employee it is likely that part of your job will be concerned with completing or processing a range of forms on a regular basis. You are usually trained in their use and after a short period of time, this becomes a matter of routine. Admittedly, some members of the public, who have frequent bank transactions may become equally familiar with your forms but there is always a large group who may use specific services infrequently and therefore will find banking procedures, and the forms that support these procedures, strange. For instance if you operate a computer terminal every day you may be used to inputting information from a form using an optical character reader but the client who has to complete the information on the form may find this particular layout bewildering if not alarming. The kinds of questions which spring to his/her mind when confronted with a form of this description are: Does every box have to have a character in it? Can you cross out a mistake? Will the computer understand what I have written? If you are at the counter you may have to answer these questions for the customer.

Importance of Accurate Forms

Whatever type of form is being used and whoever is involved in completing it, the information will only be of value to the bank if it is accurate and complete. If there are blank spaces on the form, if information is inserted in the wrong place or is obviously incomplete it will cost the bank time and money trying to rectify the situation.

As a bank employee, you may be able to play an important role in ensuring that forms are accurate and complete:

- If you are in direct contact with the public and issue forms for them to complete, offer assistance in completing them if they appear hesitant or worried; it is worthwhile to spend a few moments at this stage on something you may think is very simple but which a client finds perplexing.

- If your job is to receive forms from the public, scan their entries on the spot to detect any obvious errors or omissions, e.g. blank spaces, no signature or date; again, it is better to spend a few moments on scanning at the counter than to allow an incorrect form through to a later stage in processing. It will hold up such procedures and, further more, any delay may upset the client.

- If you complete internal forms make sure that you have followed the instructions for completion correctly and that you check the information you are inserting for accuracy — don't get over-confident, reckoning that you can do the job without giving it your full attention. If you do, you are sure to make a mistake at the worst possible time!

- If your job involves checking entries on forms, or transferring information from one form to another, ensure that you give this task your full attention. Do not regard it as an annoying inconvenience.

Forms and the Client

ACTIVITY 3

Pause for Thought

Have any of your organisation's clients ever commented on your forms? If so, have these comments been complimentary or derogatory? Have they expressed difficulties in completing them?

As mentioned earlier, your bank's forms may be part of your daily routine but for the client they may present problems. Clients' attitudes to official forms may well affect the efficiency with which they complete them. Let's examine some problems clients may experience:

- You may have clients whose accounts may be in a sound financial state but who may have limited reading or writing ability. They may try to avoid having to fill in forms or may refuse to do so.

- Some may find the official language that appears on many forms difficult to understand and therefore they get flustered and do not fill in the form correctly. Remember that banking forms are designed by bankers who are familiar with banking terminology. It is unfair to expect members of the public to understand the same language as readily (see Chapter 1, page 9, on importance of designing communication for the receiver).

- Some may become anxious about what information to include and what to omit. For instance, if the instructions say 'Full name', do they have to admit to a middle name which they never use and hate.

- Some people become suspicious of the motives behind certain questions. They have heard of phrases such as 'financial status' and they view questions on a form as a series of traps designed to detect the 'worthy' from the 'unworthy'.

- Others are concerned about what financial interpretation will be put on some of their answers about life-style: 'Will the bank view my status in the right light if I admit that I am a tenant rather than an owner-occupier?'

- Some may have problems that derive from the layout of the form. For example, if the form only provides two lines for answering a question on existing credit commitments, does the client only have to identify two credit commitments or try to cram details of every credit commitment into the two lines?

Very often you can alleviate many of these anxieties by a simple offer that assistance can be provided to help a client complete the form and an assurance that confidentiality of information will be maintained. In some cases, all that is necessary is to talk through the main headings of the form and explain the reason for the questions that are asked. Once people know *why* specific questions need to be asked and answered they are less likely to develop hostile and resentful attitudes towards completion of the form. Others will need help in making every entry and this may put demands on your patience. Never simply hand out a form — always offer assistance immediately. A simple offer of 'If you have any problems with this form, please come back and ask me for help' is quite sufficient.

Forms Design

If you have first-hand knowledge of clients experiencing problems with your organisation's forms, it is worth having a good look at the forms which are causing difficulty.

If you have already detected areas which constantly cause problems to members of the public, you can foresee and answer these problems immediately and give assistance on them *when* you hand out the form — this will prevent delay or mistakes at the outset.

At your level in the organisation you will not have responsibility for the redesign of business forms but you may be able to pass on useful comments to your superiors which could contribute to improvements in design. Aspects which you can look out for are:

(a) *Language* Are the instructions given in simple, straightforward language or is too much bank jargon used which may confuse clients?

(b) *Spacing* Is there enough space provided on the form for the information that needs to be given?

(c) *Sequence* Are questions asked in a logical progression from the point of view of the client and of the procedures for processing the information?

(d) *Typescript* Is the size of printing appropriate? Do section headings stand out conspicuously?

(e) *Instructions* Are instructions given clearly and are they located adjacent to the portion to be completed? Are clients referred to a section of the bank or to a person if they do experience difficulty in following the instructions?

Forms Control

Paperwork in banks, as in other large organisations, can run riot; forms can make a contribution to paper overload. You may have moaned from time to time that there are too many forms to complete. When tempted to moan about forms, remember that they are a systematic way of gathering essential information so that decisions can be made. Without forms the process could become even more time-consuming. Responsibility for overall control of business forms will lie elsewhere in your organisation but you can still play your part in ensuring that there is not a proliferation of unnecessary paper.

Forms are likely to be reviewed and renewed from time to time; instructions will be circulated that form . . . has been withdrawn and is now replaced by form . . .. Have you looked at such a memo and then promptly forgotten it so that you continue to use an obsolete form after its official withdrawal date? Make sure you do withdraw all out-of-date forms and leaflets from your files and from public display.

If you do find that you have been issued with forms which you do not need to use, i.e. they duplicate forms already in use or they fail to secure the right kind of information, report this to your superior so that your information can be included in the next forms review. For example, you may find on computerised forms that the layout of the information on the form is not consistent with the order in which it must be inputted to the computer.

ACTIVITY 4

Exercise

Refer back to your answer to Activity 3. Now be more specific about this and list the difficulties:

(a) which are most frequently expressed by the public;
(b) which are most frequently experienced by you.

Give as many suggestions as you can of improvements which could be made. You might like to keep these suggestions for future reference at work when they have a forms review.

Although forms present some problems, usually concerned with design, at least they do not demand the more difficult problems of composition and choice involved in letter writing. This will be considered next.

LETTERS

Of all the communication methods, this is perhaps the one which is most frequently criticised. This is not only true of the banks but of other organisations too. Somehow we all see the letter as being the primary representative of the organisation; because it is a formal communication, it carries an 'official seal of approval', whoever has written it.

Since letter writing is one of the most complex and difficult tasks in business, it is quite likely that most people will make some mistakes and these are promptly held up as examples of incompetence which reflect on the organisation as a whole. Strangely enough, however, every individual thinks that his/her own method of composing and phrasing letters is irreproachable and this perception of our own perfection has led to a situation where we find it very difficult to change our habits, however appalling these seem to other people. It is for this reason that bad practice in letter writing — the perpetuation of outdated and overworked phrases and stilted language — has persisted, particularly in bureaucratic institutions. The banks are no exception.

One of the most difficult problems for a new member of staff to combat is the *house style* — that is, the one approved by the organisation as a whole and, more importantly, by his/her immediate superior. Even if the style is poor, it is difficult to oppose it. Nevertheless, where the house style is old-fashioned, over-pompous or incomprehensible it is worth at least attempting to make some progress towards plain English. There is, after all, an organisation now devoted specifically to doing this — the Campaign for Plain English. This organisation has gone some way towards changing the style of government departments and other offenders. Again, the important principle is to write for the *receiver* and that usually means being concise and courteous.

There are many aspects which you need to consider to produce a good letter.

ACTIVITY 5

Pause for Thought

What factors do you think you should consider before writing any letter? Note these down and then check your list against the one given at the end of the chapter.

Objectives of the Letter

A letter may be required for a number of reasons. The most usual are:

- asking for information
- giving information
- making a complaint
- responding to a complaint
- asking for money
- refusing or granting approval
- persuading the reader to accept a service, idea or a course of action
- promising or threatening a specific course of action

The banks are involved in all of these letters and they will need very careful planning accordingly. They will need to take into account the receiver's likely attitudes as well as the reader's degree of familiarity with the situation or matter in hand.

Deciding clearly what the objectives are and what the reader's likely response will be, govern tone and approach of the letter and it is essential to decide these matters before any further planning takes place.

Types of Letter

The objectives which have been discussed will dictate the type of letter which is required in each situation. The composition and sequence of each one need to vary. However, let us consider the most common types of letter which you might be required to compose or answer.

Letters of Enquiry and Reply One of the most common letters which you are likely to receive, even in your early days at the bank is the letter of enquiry — usually about services which you have to offer. Such a letter will normally fall into three paragraphs:

Paragraph 1 states the purpose of the letter, i.e. what it is about.

Paragraph 2 states the background details of the reason for the enquiry and any special circumstances.

Paragraph 3 gives a final question/query/statement which indicates what action/response the writer now needs.

The response should follow very much the same kind of framework:

Paragraph 1 thanks the correspondent for the letter and acknowledges the subject of the query.

Example of a letter of enquiry

15 Willow Way,
Ockingham,
Beckhampshire 4OK 3ED.

14th May 19..

Accounts Manager,
National Eastern Bank PLC,
Market Square,
OCKINGHAM,
Beckhampshire OCK 2PG.

Dear Sir,

Personal Loans - Account Number 0657201

I have banked with your branch for the past two years. I now wish to purchase a new car and would be grateful for information on personal loans.

As I wish to purchase the car as soon as possible, I would be glad of an early reply.

Yours faithfully,

W.G. Carr

Example of a reply to a letter of enquiry

National Eastern Bank PLC

Market Square
Ockingham
Beckhampshire
OCK 2PG

Telephone: 0253 86523
Telex: NEBOCK

17 May 19..

Ref Account No 065720l

Mr W G Carr
15 Willow Way
OCKINGHAM
Beckhampshire 4OK 3ED

Dear Mr Carr

Personal Loans

Thank you for your letter dated 15 May 19.. concerning a personal loan for the purchase of a new car.

We enclose the relevant information and an application form. We would like to draw your attention to paragraph 3 in the leaflet which gives the regulations concerning loans for car purchase.

If you would like to complete the form and return it to me, we will process your application as quickly as possible.

Yours sincerely

R G Dollar
Accounts Manager

Enc Leaflet 'Personal loans'

Paragraph 2 gives the details of the reply and refers to any enclosed information or leaflets.

Paragraph 3 offers to help further and gives a contact name/number.

These letters do not present a difficult problem for you to solve. They do demand that the information you give is conscientiously checked and correct, that the language is comprehensible to a member of the public and that all the other six 'C's' discussed in Chapter 1 are observed. A more difficult letter to cope with is the letter of complaint.

Letters of Complaint Letters of complaint from the public can be politely phrased or can, on occasions, be rude, aggressive or threatening. It is worth noting that the first type often gains a better response because you feel more inclined to help the person concerned. Unfortunately, there are occasions when 'he who shouts loudest' is likely to get the quickest response to get rid of the problem! In any case, a letter of complaint usually falls into three distinct sections:

Paragraph 1 gives the reason for the complaint, briefly.

Paragraph 2 and subsequent paragraphs give details of the nature of the problem and the justification for the complaint.

Final paragraph demands/threatens action and indicates what steps the customer is likely to take if the right action from you is not forthcoming.

The important aspect to remember about the response to a letter of complaint is that however aggressive it may be, you are required to remain distanced and while not becoming personally involved, to put the matter right as quickly and competently as possible. If the complaint is not justified then a tactful explanation is required which gives the necessary information without becoming patronising. The normal sequence of response to a letter of complaint is:

Paragraph 1 acknowledges the receipt of the letter and either apologises briefly for the matter or, if the complaint is not justified, states there is an explanation for the situation.

Paragraph 2 gives reasons for the situation arising without incriminating colleagues in the organisation.

Paragraph 3 states what action will now be taken to rectify the matter or, if necessary, explains further.

Final paragraph gives an immediate contact point for any further correspondence/discussion (if necessary).

Example of a letter of complaint

22 Church Avenue,
Pilsbury,
Beckhampshire 6OK 2WP

19th January 19..

Accounts Manager,
National Eastern Bank PLC,
Market Square,
OCKINGHAM,
Beckhampshire OCK 2PG.

Dear Sir,

Standing Order to Ferguson's Stores Ltd.

On December 5th 19.. I telephoned you with a request to cancel the above standing order and you agreed to do so. However, I note from my recent bank statement that a further payment of £30 was paid on December 30th.

As the hire purchase agreement with Ferguson's had come to an end this caused me considerable inconvenience and expense in attempting to reclaim the money from them.

Will you please ensure that no further payments are made to Ferguson's Stores Ltd. and that the standing order is cancelled immediately.

Yours faithfully,

H.P. Owen

Example of a reply to a letter of complaint

National Eastern Bank PLC

Market Square
Ockingham
Beckhampshire
OCK 2PG

Telephone: 0253 86523
Telex: NEBOCK

Ref SD/PCW

21 January 19..

Mr H P Owen
22 Church Avenue
PILBURY
Beckhampshire 6OK 2WP

Dear Mr Owen

Standing Order No 16785/OWE

Thank you for your letter dated 19 January 19.. concerning the standing order to Ferguson's Stores Ltd. We apologise for the inconvenience caused by the further payment made on the above standing order.

When you telephoned, you should have been requested to confirm your request to cancel in writing. We do not appear to have received any confirmation and therefore continued to make payments. Now that we have received your letter, we have cancelled the standing order as requested.

We are sorry that you have been put to the trouble of reclaiming the money and note that the hire purchase agreement is now terminated.

Yours sincerely

S O Dunn
Accounts Manager

The discussion in Chapter 2 concerning awkward customers and complaints applies just as much in written communication. You should not grovel but should apologise briefly and should concentrate on putting the specific matter to rights. If the complaint is unjustified you should offer an explanation rather than attempt to prove a member of the public wrong.

Letters with an Unwelcome Message These are, in many ways, the most difficult to write without giving offence. They include such delicate situations as refusing overdrafts and loans, and reminders of overdue payments.

The initial letter should always bear in mind the receiver's likely attitude to the message and that a genuine error or misunderstanding may have occurred. In the case of a refusal of overdraft or loan facilities the reasons may be various: the client's unsatisfactory financial status, changes in government regulations, or unavailability of funds for the purpose required. In any case, if the answer is to be 'No' to a customer who obviously wants/needs this service, there is no point in making the situation worse by adopting an inappropriate tone or approach.

As in any situation which requires tact, it is more diplomatic to give an explanation of the reasons at some length and without denigrating the client on a personal basis before stating the decision to refuse. The sequence of the initial letter should be as follows:

Paragraph 1 acknowledges receipt of the requesting letter or raises the matter at issue. It gives a sentence which allows for the fact that a genuine mistake may have been made.

Paragraph 2 gives reasons behind the bank's response and gives relevant details of the account and/or regulations concerned in terms that are inoffensive and impartial.

Paragraph 3 demonstrates concern for the customer's case but gives a clear decision (albeit perhaps reluctantly at this stage).

Final paragraph indicates what immediate action will be taken/is required and gives a contact person/number for any response/discussion.

The tone and approach of a letter of this kind should always be helpful and diplomatic. If later follow-up letters are required, then the need for a different approach of an increasingly firm nature may be required. At this stage, however, the channels of negotiation should be left open!

Other Types of Letter Your bank may send out a variety of other letters in which you are unlikely, at this stage in your career, to be involved since the composition and design will be a matter either for a superior or for head office. Two typical examples are:

Example of a letter with an unwelcome message

National Eastern Bank PLC

Market Square
Ockingham
Beckhampshire
OCK 2PG

Telephone: 0253 86523
Telex: NEBOCK

6 January 19..

Ref PAY/PCW

Mr B Lewitt
10 Western Terrace
OCKINGHAM
Beckhampshire 4OK 5DF

Dear Mr Lewitt

Account No 656231

We wish to draw to your attention the fact that your current account is overdrawn by £250. Our overdraft arrangement with you is for a limit of £150.

We are particularly concerned because this situation seems to have arisen as a result of your salary, which is normally credited on the first of the month, not having been paid to date. Perhaps your salary payment has been delayed over the Christmas/New Year period or there is some other reason which you have not communicated to us.

We would be glad if you could contact your Account Manager, Mrs Alison Crowther, on extension 231 to explain what has occurred.

Yours sincerely

P A Yup
Assistant Manager

(a) *Confidential letters* in reply to enquiries or asking for status reports. When a customer opens a bank account, the bank sometimes needs to make status enquiries concerning credit-worthiness. Information can be obtained from the customer's own employer, from other companies with which he has had hire-purchase or loan agreements or from other banks/building societies. Normally these will concern regularity of payments, amounts of discount/credit allowed. Equally, the bank may be required to give information to other organisations concerning these aspects. The overriding concern here is for confidentiality, security, accuracy and impartiality. If you leave your bank you will need a personal reference which will have to conform to these needs, too.

(b) *Circular letters* promoting new services, where the need is to be persuasive and brief, since a long letter is unlikely to be read. These often use questions or points aimed directly at the customer, using capital letters and underlinings for emphasis to hold the reader's attention. There is usually a contact name/number at the end of the letter.

ACTIVITY 6

Pause for Thought

You might like to look at the promotional letters of your own bank and those of your competitors. Which are the most effective and why?

You might like to refer back to the points made about visual communication at the beginning of this chapter and your answers to Activity 1. The same principles will apply here.

Although various types of letter need different styles and tone you can see that they do follow a basic structure. This can be represented as follows:

Purpose
Explanation
Action

Layout

Whatever the type of letter required the rules concerning layout remain the same. Having said this, there are two quite distinct formats in use at present and you will need to check the one preferred by your bank. Whichever one is adopted, layout should be neat, consistent and professional. The two formats in use are:

(a) *Indented* This is the traditional layout which is now most usually employed for handwritten letters. Most letters from private customers are likely to have this format. The normal conventions of punctuation and paragraphing should be followed. See example and refer to Supplement 2, page 238.

(b) *Fully blocked* This format is usually adopted for formal typed/word processed letters sent out from business organisations. You are likely to experience this type of format either within your own bank or from business customers. Here, no punctuation appears in the addresses, references, dates, letter heading or in anything which appears below the last line of the letter. Paragraphs within the letter are indicated by leaving a line space and punctuation follows normal rules. See example and refer to Supplement 2, page 238.

There are also a number of mixtures of the two formats which are now accepted into general use. These are generally referred to as:

(c) *Semi-blocked* This format has much of the letter using the blocked style but some items are indented. This is sometimes preferred by business organisations. There are a variety of ways of punctuating semi-blocked letters. You will have to check your own house style for this and look at examples which follow. The three different formats are illustrated.

The examples which appear above are those of good practice rather than typical examples of common practice (see next section).

Whatever the overall format used, there are some rules on layout which need to be observed. These can be listed as follows:

- *The date* This should not be abbreviated but given in full, i.e. not 5.12.92 but 5 December 1992.

- *References* When replying to a letter or referring to a previous letter sent by you, quote relevant references. This will normally be composed of the initials of the person writing the letter and the typist or a file/account number concerning the correspondence.

- *The addressee* If you know the name of the person to whom you are writing you should quote this together with his/her job position if known. NB If you use the term 'Esq.' after a person's name you should omit 'Mr'. Both together are *never* used. Sometimes you are not aware of the name of the person concerned and you will either address your letter to the job position or department, e.g. Accounts Manager or The Standing Orders Department. Occasionally you may not know even this and will need to address the letter to the organisation.

- *Address* This should be given in full with the postal town shown in capitals and with the post code.

Example of an indented letter

18 Russley Green,
Ockingham,
Beckhampshire,
OCK 2LP.

7 March 19--

Accounts Manager,
National Eastern Bank PLC,
Market Square,
OCKINGHAM,
Beckhampshire OCK 2PG.

Dear Sir,

Account Number: 809504

I have recently moved house to the above address and although I did inform you of the move, I have not received my last bank statement.

My previous address was:

15 Kendal Avenue,
Oakshott,
Beckhampshire, OCK 5DA.

I would be grateful if you could check my change of address has been recorded on your files and send me a duplicate bank statement.

Yours faithfully,

D.A. STEVENS

Example of a fully blocked letter

Starmead Software Ltd
Holland House
Bury Way
OCKINGHAM
Beckhampshire OCK 4PD
Telephone 0253 40967
Telex STARM 3

7 March 19--

Ref MAS/SUS

Accounts Manager
National Eastern Bank PLC
Market Square
OCKINGHAM
Beckhampshire OCK 2PG

Dear Sir

Change of trading address

Please note that our address will change as from 10 March 19-- from the above to:

Starmead House
High Street
Ockingham
Beckhampshire OCK 5PC

Our account number is 903400.

We would be grateful if you could amend your records accordingly.

Yours faithfully

M STAR
Managing Director

Directors M A Star Ph D B Sc
J C Mead B Sc
P D Star FCA
Incorporated London No 125467

Example of a semi-blocked letter

National Eastern Bank PLC

Market Square
Ockingham
Beckhampshire
OCK 2PG

Telephone: 0253 86523
Telex: NEBOCK

Ref. JCW/MCP

8 March 19--

Mr. D.A. Stevens,
18 Russley Green,
OCKINGHAM,
Beckhampshire OCK 2LP.

Dear Mr. Stevens,

Account No. 809504

Thank you for your letter dated 7 March 19-- reminding us of your change of address.

Your original notification unfortunately arrived too late for the issue of your last bank statement, which must have gone to your previous address.

We enclose a duplicate bank statement for your records and hope you have not been inconvenienced.

Yours sincerely,

J.C. WHITE
Accounts Manager

Enc. Bank statement

▶ *Salutation* If you know the name of the person concerned begin with this, i.e. 'Dear Mr Stevens'. If not, use 'Dear Sir' or 'Dear Madam' (whichever is appropriate). If you do not know the sex of the receiver, use 'Dear Sir or Madam'. Occasionally you may have to write a letter to a woman whose name you know but you are not sure whether she is Mrs or Miss. In this case Ms can be used.

▶ *Letter heading* Any business letter should contain a heading which summarises the subject of the letter. This ensures that it:

(a) goes to the right person;
(b) focuses the attention of the reader on the matter in hand;
(c) refers them to the relevant records or files.

▶ *Complimentary close* If you have used the person's name, 'Yours sincerely' is the correct close. Otherwise it is 'Yours faithfully'.

▶ *Signature* This should appear below the complimentary close and should always be followed by the typed (or printed) name of the sender since most signatures are illegible. If you are a woman it is helpful to indicate Mrs or Miss in brackets. In your early days at the bank you may have to sign on behalf of your superior or leave a space for his/her signature and you should check what is required. If you are required to sign a letter on his/her behalf you should put *your* usual signature and then put the letters p.p. before *his/her* typed name.

▶ *Enclosures* If there are any enclosures the letters Enc. or Encs. should appear against the left-hand margin together with the titles of the enclosures listed. This enables enclosures to be checked before despatch and on arrival.

▶ *Correct form of address* Occasionally you may have to address a letter to people who have a decoration, degrees or a title. The correct form is to show decorations and then degrees, e.g. A.T. Lake, OBE., MA. Correct forms of address for people with titles and members of the clergy can be found in the reference book, Black's *Titles and Forms of Address.*

Language

The language and style adopted should be plain and understandable. Outdated phrases and ungrammatical constructions are unfortunately widespread but they are to be avoided at all costs. Some of the most common errors and/or bad practice, together with some suggested improvements, are given below:

Beginning and Ending Letters

(a) Many people begin letters with the phrase 'I am writing this letter to . . .'. This is obvious and the words should therefore be omitted.

(b) Participle constructions to begin or end letters, e.g. 'Referring to your letter.'; 'Awaiting your reply'. Neither of these is a complete sentence. In the first instance 'referring' is a participle only and not a main verb (see page 230). The phrase should therefore be followed by a comma and not a full stop and the sentence should be continued, e.g. 'Referring to your letter of 6 April, we have now changed our records.' In the second instance, words ending in 'ing' should always be avoided at the end of a letter and a complete sentence should be given instead, e.g. 'I hope to hear from you soon.'

Outdated Expressions These are sometimes known as 'officialese' which is very stilted. Some examples of these expressions and their modern preferred phrases are shown below:

Not this	*but possibly this*
We acknowledge receipt of	Thank you for
We have pleasure in	We are happy to
We note your comments regarding	You mention that
Enclosed please find Enclosed herewith Attached please find	I am enclosing
Awaiting the favour of your reply	We hope to hear from you soon
Please do not hesitate to	Please
Thanking you in advance	(Omit)
Regretting our inability to be of service	(Omit)
Trusting we may be favoured by a prompt reply	(Omit)
As per	According to
Re	About (NB omit Re in letter headings)
Viz	Namely
The undersigned	I
Our Mr Black	Mr Black, our representative
May we take this opportunity Allow me to say Permit me to say	(In all cases get on and do it and omit these phrases!)
In the not too distant future	Before long or soon
In due course	(Be more specific) Within a few days/weeks/months
At the present time	Now
At a later date	Later
Yours of recent date	Your letter dated

The following verbose phrases should be shortened

Not this	*but possibly this*
Due to the fact that	Because/as
In the event that	If
On the occasion of	When
With regard to In respect of	About
Prior to	Before
In the neighbourhood of	Near
With a view to For the purpose of In order to	To
According to our records	We find
Answer in the affirmative/ negative	Say yes/no

It is *not* good letter style to use as many long words as possible or to adopt a flowery or journalistic approach. The guiding principle can be summed up as follows:

Keep
It
Short and
Simple

To observe this principle, one discipline which can be imposed is to reduce what has come to be known as the *fog factor*— that is the degree of complexity of any piece of written English. The fog factor is calculated by counting the number of words on a page with three syllables or more and then counting the number of sentences on the page. The calculation is

$$\frac{\text{number of words (3 syllables or more)}}{\text{number of sentences}} = \text{fog factor}$$

You should aim at a fog factor of 3 or less if you are to be understood clearly.

Letters are a common method of communication but they are not always as effective as they might be because the simple principles discussed in this chapter have not been observed.

ACTIVITY 7

Exercise

The following letter contains a variety of out-dated or verbose phrases which contribute to a high fog factor.

Dear Sir,

We are in receipt of your communication of 5.6.87. We note your dissatisfaction regarding the unsatisfactory situation which you have given in your commentary and which concerned our procedures in computerising your bank statements.

We note that following your perusal of your recent statement you were of the opinion that it was illegible and incomprehensible.

It will be appreciated that computerisation assists our organisation in the speed of its transactions. In the not too distant future we may, however, conduct an evaluation of the current situation and review the reactions both affirmative and negative of our customers.

Regretting our inability to be of service but assuring you of our best attention at all times.

Yours faithfully,

Check the fog factor. Then make your own improvements to the letter and recalculate the fog factor. You will find one revised letter at the end of the chapter.

AIDS TO GOOD LETTER WRITING

The production of correspondence on word processors in modern offices enables you to use a range of facilities which should help your letter writing. These include:

- ability to produce the template for a fully blocked letter layout on screen
- a choice of type fonts
- the availability of spell-checkers on most software (If your software does not have a good *English* spellcheck, then make sure you have a good dictionary by your side.)

- the availability of a thesaurus on some software (If your software does not have a thesaurus, buy one of the paperback editions and keep it by your side so that you can use a range of vocabulary and make your letters less boring.)
- the ability to proof read letters on screen to check content, layout and style before printing.

Use Supplement 2 at the end of this book to help you with any difficulties over sentence construction or punctuation.

To assist you in your letter writing here are two check-lists:

DON'T

- use jargon, officialese or outdated phrases
- allow a high fog factor
- be long-winded
- be condescending, rude or over-familiar
- allow a letter to leave the organisation without checking for errors in layout, punctuation, spelling or sentence construction

DO

- bear in mind the purpose of your letter
- plan a logical sequence
- use simple, direct vocabulary and sentences
- ensure your letter is complete, clear, concise and courteous
- remember that your letter represents your organisation
- check any letter for errors
- remember the key words for:

Structure

Purpose
Explanation
Action

and Style

Keep
It
Short and
Simple

It is quite likely that at present you may produce a rought draft of any letter or memo which needs to be typed. Later you may have the services of a shorthand or audio typist so you should know something of the skills of dictation. Many people are very bad at dictating on to cassette — ask any audio typist!

DICTATION

ACTIVITY 8

Pause for Thought

If you are friendly with any audio or shorthand typists, ask them about some of the annoying habits of the managers who give them dictation.

Some of the faults they might identify are:

- Giving special instructions relating to the dictation *at the end* of the passage.
- Dictating while smoking or chewing so that the words are indistinct.
- Walking round the office away from the recorder so that the voice fades from time to time.
- Dictating while a riot is going on in the office!
- Failing to spell difficult proper names, technical terms.

These are only a few faults. So that you do not get blacklisted as a poor dictator, use the following guidelines to develop your skill:

Preparation

- Assemble the documents you need and make notes of the main points you want to include.
- Dictate at a time and in a place where there will be a minimum of background noise.

Initial Instructions

- Give a greeting which identifies your name, department and extension number (unless the typist works exclusively for you).
- Specify the following:

(a) type of document;
(b) approximate length (or size of paper);
(c) number of copies required;
(d) instructions concerning distribution of copies;
(e) instructions on any special layout;
(f) any documents/files which may be needed for reference.

Sequence

Dictate information in the sequence in which it appears in a letter or memo. In the early days it is a good idea to have a sample letter or memo in front of you as you dictate for guidance.

General Guidelines

Pace and audibility

▶ Check the volume/tone controls on the recorder and practise to find the right volume and tone for *your* voice.

▶ Pronounce words clearly.

▶ Use natural phrasing, pausing at commas and at the ends of sentences.

▶ Try to avoid dropping your voice at the ends of words or sentences.

Punctuation and paragraphing commands

▶ These should *precede* the dictation, e.g. open bracket . . . close bracket, or paragraph one . . . paragraph two. . . .

▶ Dictate any punctuation you think is necessary. If you have confidence in the typist, then dictate only unusual punctuation. If you are in doubt, dictate each comma, full stop and capital letter.

Spelling It helps the typist if you spell proper names, foreign or unusual words. Since some letters sound the same when dictated, e.g. p/b, t/d, it is useful to use the phonetic alphabet. This was given on page 32.

Numbers Some of these are easily confused, e.g. 50/15, so dictate five 0 or one five.

Corrections When you make mistakes and have to go back and re-record, make sure you begin at exactly the right point and make sure you have not wiped out any information in error.

Pause/stop buttons If you over-use these you will get a very jerky delivery; you will find that practice will overcome this.

CONCLUSION

In this chapter we have considered the most common ways in which a bank communicates with the public in written form. The major principle, whether composing a letter or helping a member of the public with a form, is that you need to achieve a clean understanding on their part and that they are left with the impression that you are efficient and professional but above all that you care about their problem. If this is achieved then the image of the bank and its public relations will be well presented — and this is what the organisation really needs from you.

SUGGESTED ANSWERS TO ACTIVITIES

Activity 5

Factors you might have noted are:

(a) objectives of the letter — to inform, complain etc.;
(b) type of letter and appropriate structure/content;
(c) layout of letter — blocked, indented etc.;
(d) language, style, approach and tone appropriate to the situation.

Activity 7

Thank you for your letter of the 5th April. We are sorry that you find your computerised statements difficult to read and understand.

The bank uses a computer for a faster and more efficient service. Soon, however, we will review our service in the light of customers' reactions.

We are sorry we cannot change the situation immediately but assure you that we do note customers' comments.

(Reduced to a fog factor of 2.)

ASSIGNMENT

Write a reply to the following letter of complaint. More detailed instructions will appear at the end of the letter.

13 Church Avenue,
OCKINGHAM,
Beckhampshire
0CK 9WL.

3rd April 19..

Accounts Manager,
National Eastern Bank PLC,
Market Square,
OCKINGHAM,
Beckhampshire 0CK 2PG.

Dear Sir,

I am writing this letter to complain about the cash dispensing machines at your bank.

I have a very difficult job which does not allow me to visit the bank during normal banking hours — except on very rare occasions. Therefore I have to use the cash dispenser quite frequently. Nine times out of ten when I try to use it in the evenings or at weekends, I find it closed. This is very unsatisfactory.

There must be many people like me who find that bank services are not geared to their needs. Why are the banks open at such ridiculous hours? Couldn't you have an evening session? Even on the occasions when I have rushed in at lunchtime, half the bank tellers seem to be out at lunch. The queues have been so long that I have had to leave before my turn arrived. This must be a peak time. Why don't you employ more rather than less staff at these times? If you can't do this, surely it is not beyond the wit and intelligence of the bank to fill up the cash dispenser to last 12 hours!

I would like an answer to these questions. If I do not get a reasonable answer I shall have to think seriously about taking my account to another bank.

Yours, in frustration,

P.W. Scroggins

You will note that this letter is a typical one containing many errors usual in communications from the public. It is therefore *not* an example of good letter writing.

The letter has been passed to you to draft a reply for your superior, the Accounts Manager, to sign. Your reply should be a model of good practice using appropriate language, tone and correct fully blocked layout.

PART 3

Communication and Information Technology

4 New Developments in Telecommunications

In the preceding chapters we have examined basic forms of communication in business — oral and written — and made some reference to the use of computers and telecommunications in aiding such communication. The convergence of microprocessor and telecommunications technologies has enabled us to use a wide range of communications options to transmit speech, text, data and image. Such developments are particularly important in financial institutions which are branch based and where rapid and accurate communication between Head Office, regions and branches is vital to remain competitive. This chapter will discuss some of the technological developments which are affecting business communication today.

TELEPHONE

In Chapter 2 we discussed telephone techniques when dealing with members of the public. The telephone is also a useful medium for all kinds of communication within and between organisations. It is so easy to pick up a telephone and transact our business.

ACTIVITY 1

Pause for Thought

Why do you think the telephone is so popular and important a means of communication?

The popularity of the telephone and the realisation of the vital role it has to play in business has contributed to a vast updating of our telephone network to cope with the demands of industry and commerce. The privatisation of British Telecom has meant that there are other telecommunications manufacturers now competing to provide a wide range of telephone systems.

Many organisations have a *private branch exchange* (PBX), otherwise referred to as a switchboard. This accepts calls and transfers them to appropriate extensions. You will find that today large organisations, such as banks, building societies, etc. will have a *computerised automatic branch exchange* (CABX) with a range of sophisticated features. This type of switchboard is electronic and can be programmed to provide a range of services. On the more sophisticated CABX systems these would include:

- *Abbreviated dialling and number storage* — a facility which enables frequently used numbers to be stored on memory and then to be dialled by an abbreviated two button code.

- *Alarm calls* — a facility which allows an extension user to arrange for a call to be made at a given time as a reminder for important meetings, etc.

- *Amplified speech* — a facility which enables a call to be heard across a room.

- *Automatic ring back* — a facility which allows the system to ring the extension user when a contact has been made with a number that was previously unobtainable.

- *Break in facility* — a facility which enables the system to interrupt a conversation in the case of an emergency or urgent call for that extension.

- *Call barring* — a facility to restrict the range of connections on a particular extension, e.g. could be used to bar external calls, trunk calls or international calls, etc.

- *Call divert* — a facility which allows a call to be diverted automatically to another extension/s if the original extension is engaged or the member of staff does not want to be disturbed.

- *Call forwarding* — a facility for giving programmed instructions for incoming calls to be routed via specific extensions to find a mobile member of staff.

- *Call hold* — a facility for keeping a line open to a caller while a member of staff is being found, or while the extension is being used to check information internally.

- *Call logging* — a facility for maintaining a record of all outgoing and, if necessary, incoming calls from/to specific extensions.

- *Conference calls* — a facility which enables several extension users to talk to one another over the telephone and to include an outside caller, if necessary.

- *Dictation access* — a facility which enables an extension to be connected with a central dictation service.

- *Direct inward dialling* — a facility which enables incoming calls to be routed directly to an extension without going through an operator by adding the extension number to the normal organisation's number.

- *Direct outward dialling* — a facility which allows outgoing calls to have direct access to the Public Switched Telephone Network.

- *Last number redial* — a facility which stores the last number dialled by an extension user automatically so that the number can be redialled by merely pressing the redial number.

- *Music on hold* — a facility for playing music immediately an incoming call is put on hold.

Most CABX systems will feature a series of ringing codes or flashing buttons which the system operator can use to indicate to extension users whether a line is busy, when a call is waiting to be connected, when they have been connected to an outside line or when a number dialled is unobtainable. A CABX also allows the organisation to programme individual handsets. Some may have the full range of facilities; others may have certain facilities barred.

Other organisations may have a *keysystem*. This is generally suitable for smaller organisations which do not need a switchboard operator. It is another electronic telephone system which enables any telephone extension to accept an incoming call and to route it to an alternative. This is done by linking the extension units in a circuit. Often one member of staff, e.g. a secretary, will have answering incoming calls as a priority duty.

Mobile Telephones

Since many managers need to be in constant contact with their offices when on the move, there has been a rapid growth in the use of the cellular telephone network. Some mobile telephones can be fitted permanently in cars so that they are powered by the car battery; others, usually referred to as transportables, operate from their own batteries.

Radio signals from these telephones are picked up by a transmitter in the local area (referred to as a cell) and transferred to the Public Switched Telephone Network. As the unit moves from one cell to another the call is interrupted (without loss of contact to the caller) and the call transmitted by the next cell's transmitter. Cellular phones are now available in some forms of public transport (i.e. some trains and planes) so that business people can remain in touch.

BT Services

As a user of the telephone and a member of a public service you should also be aware of the services offered by British Telecom (BT) to all telephone users. These services include:

- *ADC* (Advice of Duration and Charge) — you make most calls at home and abroad by direct dialling using standard trunk dialling and international direct dialling. However, if you want to record the duration and the charge for a particular call, it is possible to ask the operator for an ADC call.

- *Audio conferencing* — BT can provide a regional, national or international telephone link for important meetings.

- *Citicall* — This is a BT information service on stocks and shares.

- *Credit cards* — These can be issued to individuals or organisations and are another move towards eliminating the need for coins when using public telephones. The caller gives the number of his/her credit card when making a call and the charge is made to the telephone account of the person or organisation authorising the credit.

- *Fixed time calls* — It is possible to "book" a telephone call in advance with the operator so that the call will be put through at a specific time.

- *"Freefone" service* — This facility enables callers to make free telephone calls to an organisation by dialling a special freefone number. It is useful both for customers or clients and for employees working away from the organisation.

- *Radio paging* — It is possible for individuals to be "bleeped" anywhere in the country by a radio signal which requests them to get into telephone contact with their office. Some will only emit a tone bleep, others will display an LCD message.

ACTIVITY 2

Exercise

(a) Check the telephone system in your own organisation to see which of the above facilities it possesses.

(b) If you discover any facilities of which you were unaware, find out *exactly* how they work so that you can use them efficiently.

For other services your local telephone directory is a very useful source of information. It is worth looking at the introductory pages and noting the kind of information they contain. Remember that some members of the public view banks as general information centres and expect you to be able to answer all kinds of queries.

Despite the simplicity and convenience of using a modern telephone it has limitations; consequently other systems have been developed to overcome these disadvantages.

ACTIVITY 3

Pause for Thought

Try to identify some of the disadvantages of using the telephone for business communication from your own experience.

One of the disadvantages you may have noted is the time and effort you waste sitting on the end of a phone trying to establish contact or when you get through you find that the person you need to speak to is not available. Admittedly modern CABX systems limit these frustrations but, even so, there are likely to be times when the CABX console and/or extensions are not manned. At these times a telephone answering system may be useful.

Telephone Answering Systems

Answering Machines The installation of a telephone answering machine enables incoming telephone messages to be recorded out of office hours when the switchboard is not attended. However, many callers are disconcerted by such answering machines and either ring off without leaving any message or leave an inadequate message. It is therefore important that you are able to leave a complete but concise message. This is why the preparation for making a telephone call (Chapter 2, pages 32–3) is essential. Talking to an answering machine is one-way communication and there is no one to prompt you at the other end about any ambiguities or omissions. You must provide the following in a *clear voice*:

- your name
- the name of your organisation and department/section
- your telephone number and extension
- the nature of your business
- what action you want the receiver to take
- a close

Telephone Answering Service Many local information bureaux provide a facility for accepting and relaying telephone messages to businesses whose employees must be away from the office for a length of time.

BT offer a Voicebank 24 hour computerised telephone message service. There are various voicebank centres which will store telephone messages at your own "mailbox" on the computer. Messages can be sent or accessed using a personal voicebox telephone number and a keypad. A mailbox can store 48 one-minute messages at a time, so once again the ability to leave a concise message is vital.

ACTIVITY 4

Exercise

Assume that you are calling a business client about a query, e.g. about a standing order or direct debit detail or to arrange an appointment for an interview. Choose a situation which is closely related to your own work. When you establish contact with the number you are connected to an answering machine and you are asked to leave a message.

Write out in full the message you would leave to include all the information listed above.

ALTERNATIVES TO THE TELEPHONE

A further disadvantage of the telephone as a means of communication is that there is no written record of a telephone conversation other than the notes you may have made. In various business transactions you may have to follow up a telephone conversation by posting letters, documents or statistics to the person. Today alternatives are available that enable you to provide an exchange of text, data or image within a matter of minutes, if not seconds, avoiding the delay involved in conventional post.

Telegrams and Telemessages

One alternative to the telephone if you want a written message to be received more promptly than by conventional mail is to use an international telegram (if overseas) or a telemessage (if in this country). Both services are offered by BT and can be used by dialling 100 on the telephone and asking for either the telemessage service or international telegrams. A telegram will be transmitted using the BT Integrated Services Digital Network to a local exchange and then delivered immediately it is received. A telemessage will be transmitted over BT's Datel circuits to computer printing terminals, where it enters the Royal Mail for delivery by first class post the next morning. Both telegrams and telemessages are charged by the number of words in the message and it is therefore vital to be concise. An example of a telegram is shown on page 85.

Example of a telegram

British TELECOM for enquiries dial the number shown in your dialling instructions

T 1291

Telegram for enquiries dial the number shown in your dialling instructions

British

21 JAN 1990/2352

ZCZC CLN7779 LAW588 LOS017 IBX1/003

GBXX CO NGIB 039

IBADAN 39/37 19 1103

MR. J. WHITE DEPT BUSINESS STUDIES

OCKINGHAM COLL OF TECH OCKINGHAM BECKHANTS OCK 2PG

UNABLE TO RETURN COLLEGE DUE TO SICKNESS HOPE TO RESUME

FEB 1

ROTIMI OLUBORODE

Telex

Many of the new systems to be mentioned in this section require you to be a subscriber to the system, i.e. pay a subscription fee. Telex is one example. The word telex is short for telegraphic exchange (of messages). It is a worldwide service offered by BT which enables written messages to be sent from one telex subscriber to another. You have probably seen the telex number of an organisation recorded together with the telephone and FAX number on the organisation's headed paper.

At one time it was necessary to have dedicated terminals known as teleprinters to send and receive telex messages. If you have such a terminal, it will be able to store and recall keyed in text and messages, provide a text editing feature (very much like any word processing package) as well as sending and receiving messages at pre-determined times. The service is available 24 hours a day and a teleprinter, once switched on, can transmit and receive messages even when not attended. This means that you are not dependent on your business contact being in the office at the precise moment that you send your message. Any message will be printed at both the sender's and the receiver's teleprinter, so both have an identical record of the exchange of information.

BT have a standard rental charge for hiring the teleprinter equipment and a line to a telex exchange. However, software has now been developed which allows an operator to use the telex service directly from a desk top personal computer using a telex link. BT are now promoting terminals with an electronic mailbox facility which can be linked to computer workstations and bring telex facilities to the desk of the busy manager. These developments have taken place as a result of the intensive competition from facsimile transfer (see page 87).

Charges for the transmission of messages are based on the distance between the caller and receiver and on the duration of the call; therefore telex messages should not involve long rambling sentences. Since time is money, you should be clear, complete and concise and it is worth editing the text to achieve this. An annotated example of a telex message is shown below to help you.

Annotated telex message

87-08-12 16:22	Date and time
007	
*AB179 16.22**	
311890 MGPUBS G	Code of sender
KEY+7170842+	Code of receiver
ERNEX AA170842	
311890 MGPUBS G	Transaction number
3462 87-08-12 16:23	Date and time repeated

ATTN CHRIS PLAYER

RE: PARADIGM DISTRIBUTION IN AUSTRALIA

I RECEIVED MESSAGE THAT YOU AGREE TO REPRESENT PARADIGM BUT AM AWAITING CONFIRMATION BY POST. I WOULD LIKE TO INCLUDE ASTAM. PLEASE ADVISE.

REGARDS
ADAM MARSHALL
PARADIGM PUBLISHING

(Message)

*	
ERNEX AA170842	Code of sender repeated
311890 MGPUBS G	Code of receiver repeated

ACTIVITY 5

Exercise

You want to send a message quickly to the Jersey branch of National Eastern Bank PLC. Your telex number is 563289 and your telex code name is NATEST G. You are sending the message at the end of the working day on Monday 25 June 19.. at 6.00 p.m. so that the Jersey branch (456880 JENAT G) can act on the information first thing on Tuesday morning.

You want to send the message to the Account Manager Mr P. Leblanc. He had requested earlier in the day a credit reference for one of your clients, Ms Josephine Cottrell, who is conducting business in Jersey. You wish to reply that her credit rating is good.

Write out in full the information that would be shown on the telex, including a suitable reply to the request.

If you have any difficulties with the layout, look at the annotated example of a telex message on page 86.

You can always compare your finished version with the one that appears at the end of the chapter.

OTHER USES OF THE TELEPHONE NETWORK

We tend to think of the telephone network as a facility for transmitting speech. In fact, using the new telecommunications systems it is possible to transmit text and data.

Electronic Jotters

These electrowriter systems transmit handwritten messages and hand-drawn diagrams or pictures to receivers. The machine is attached to a telephone and once a telephone link has been made, and a switch pressed, it is possible to write on the jotter with a special pen. Whatever is written is reproduced on a similar machine at the other end. It is therefore possible for identical permanent written records to be made of a telephone conversation for the caller and receiver.

Facsimile Transfer (FAX)

Facsimile transfer, referred to commonly as FAX, has developed widely in the last few years for transferring all kinds of messages — reports, important letters, maps, diagrams, photographs, contracts. FAX equipment, known as transceivers, can transmit and receive messages and are given a rating according to the speed at which the transmission takes place. For example, a group 2 FAX can take 6 minutes to transmit or receive an A4 business letter. Group 3 will carry out the task in about 20 seconds. Group 4, developed in Japan, can take about 6 seconds! Group 2 and 3 machines can "talk" to one another but only at group 2 speeds.

A FAX transceiver converts the original document for transmission into a series of electronic signals so that it can be transmitted via a telecommunications network (or satellite radio). At the receiving end a compatible transceiver will convert the signals back into their original form. There is an inbuilt modem in the transceiver to convert signals. Messages can be transmitted over public telephone networks, private lines or satellites.

FAX machines have a sophisticated range of features such as:

- automatic call initiation
- automatic storage of last number dialled
- automatic copying of transmitted documents
- storage of a number of messages for transmission at predetermined transmission times
- reception polling which enables a receiver to accept an incoming message once a password has been passed to the transmitter (for confidentiality)
- ability to transmit a message to a number of FAX machines once passwords have been exchanged
- tone indicators to show ringing, engaged, unobtainable
- provision of a printout listing the number of calls made, date, time, transmission time, etc.

Data links

It is also possible to send computer data via the telephone network using data links. To use the telephone network it is necessary to use a modem to convert the signals. The BT data system is known as Datel although private data transmission systems can be developed between sites or organisations.

Videotex

This term is applied internationally to interactive services which enable a user to access a central database using the telephone network, a modem, a monitor and a keyboard. In this country BT has used the term *viewdata* to refer to such services. Companies can develop their own private viewdata systems as can research organisations, libraries, etc. The public system is known as *Prestel*.

Information for Prestel is provided by a wide range of public and private organisations and this information is stored on the Prestel central computer. It is arranged in pages, each of which is a screenful of information. Information providers can update their pages and create new ones.

Those accessing Prestel for information do so by establishing a telephone link and keying in an identity number and password. A menu system enables the appropriate topics and pages to be accessed using the keyboard. It is also interactive in that it allows the user to carry out certain transactions once information has been located. Prestel's interactive facilities has been used to provide a home banking facility as well as similar arrangements for travel and entertainment bookings, hotel reservations, etc.

It is also possible to use Prestel to access private computerised databases via "gateways". A gateway is a term used to describe an electronic network which links two remote computers to the user. An additional fee is charged for this service.

Private versions of Prestel are used by large organisations, or groups of organisations, for their own purposes. Travel agents and tour operators have a videotex system for hotel and flight bookings. A videotex system is also used by city finance houses to pass on current share prices to dealers.

ACTIVITY 6

Pause for Thought

Does your branch use either Datel links or Fax to communicate with other branches or head office? If so, what kind of information is transmitted? If these systems are not used it might be worthwhile discussing with a senior colleague or a superior whether such communications systems have been considered within your organisation.

OTHER TELECOMMUNICATION NETWORKS

Most of the communications systems mentioned so far can use the telephone network referred to as the *Public Switched Telephone Network (PSTN).* The development of modern electronic equipment placed this network under excessive pressure in the 1970s and since then new networks have been developed to link electronic equipment. The original telephone network was unable to cope because once a telephone link has been established, the line opened up between caller and receiver was engaged for as long as the transaction took place (whether voice, text or data). More transactions meant more telephone lines.

Consequently BT and other telecommunications providers have developed new networks to deal with the heavier traffic.

Public Switched Network (PSS)

This system allows for the transmission of computerised data at very high speeds via telephone lines or satellite. This has enabled organisations with scattered branches to centralise information processing on a central mainframe.

Intergrated Services Digital Network (ISDN)

This is the latest network to be developed (launched in 1985) and has joined together the Public Switched Telephone Network with the Packet Switched Services so that voice, text, image or data can become fully exchangeable through a single telecommunication network. It is this network that has allowed the potential of the multi purpose electronic workstation using E-mail, FAX or telex to be realised.

Satellite communication

At one time cabling was needed for transmitting signals by most telecommunications systems. Today satellites can be used for international business communication. The public network, *Satstream*, operates by using large earth stations to direct signals at a satellite. The signals are bounced back to another point on the earth's surface to one or more receiving aerials.

Smaller dish aerials can be located on an organisation's premises or even on transport to provide private satellite links which are capable of transmitting high speed digital signals. These organisations can use this Satstream service for international telephone links, data transmissions, telex and FAX. For example it is of value to financial institutions for transacting international business, money transfers and transmitting up-to-date exchange rates, and stocks and shares prices. A form of communication which can benefit from PSS or Satstream is *teleconferencing.* This means holding a conference by means of a closed circuit TV system. BT operates a TV conferencing system known as *Confravision* through special TV studios located in various parts of the country. More recently they have offered a portable Videostream facility with a portable TV camera and a monitor which can be used in an ordinary office. This enables an organisation to conduct a national or international conference from its own premises, incorporating data links and FAX as well as the teleconferencing.

Within organisations, new networking developments have been taking place.

Local Area Networks (LANs)

These networks are made up of cable links which can transmit data or electronic messages from one terminal to another in a circuit which covers a limited area, e.g. a single branch. The terminals on the network can be any form of office electronic equipment, e.g. a personal computer, a printer, a graphics plotter, an intelligent photocopier or a FAX machine. This means that messages or data can be sent quickly round the organisation.

An LAN network can also provide instant access to a worldwide network of telecommunications services via gateways or modems for sending and receiving FAX, telex, etc. The use of LANs and access to wider systems means that a manager can transact a wide range of business from the computer terminal on his or her own desk, e.g. from composing a report, editing it, controlling the printing of copies for internal use and sending copies to other locations through the FAX service. The software packages that can be used on LANs cover a wide range of uses. These include:

- *Electronic mail* (E-mail) — a system for distributing messages from one terminal to others using in-tray and out-tray features. The messages can involve text, data or image.
- *Word processing* packages for correspondence, reports, etc.
- *Database packages* for creating and maintaining localised records or for accessing centralised records.
- *Spreadsheet packages* for forecasting, accounts, etc.
- *Graphics packages* to produce charts, graphs, line drawings, etc.
- *General management information packages* which may include electronic diaries, appointments, meeting schedules, etc.
- *Applications software suited to finance institutions,* e.g. for determining interest rates, depreciation, etc.

Wide Area Networks (WANs)

As the name implies, a WAN is a network which connects electronic equipment over a longer distance, e.g. between branches or sites within an organisation. The connection may be telephone lines or radio telecommunications.

Use of networks by financial institutions

Using new networking systems, data links enable branches scattered throughout the country to access centralised databases maintained by their bank. A terminal in a bank branch will be connected via a data link to a local computer which processes data received from a number of branches. Local processors, in turn, are linked to central mainframe computers. Likewise ATM's at banks and building societies are linked with central computers.

International payments can be made by banks using the SWIFT network *(Society* for Worldwide Interbank Financial Telecommunications) serving over a thousand banks in a wide range of countries. Electronic transfer of funds also takes place nationally between banks.

One of the latest developments which has brought together computer technology and telecommunications is the ability to transfer funds from the point of sale (e.g. shop or garage) to the bank. This system is known as *EFTPOS* (Electronic Funds Transfer from Point of Sale). A national scheme is now being implemented by EFTPOS UK, a company set up by 11 clearing banks and 3 building societies.

ACTIVITY 7

Exercise

You are working at a new high-technology branch of your bank located at the centre of the microchip and telecommunications industries. Your branch has access to all the services mentioned in the chapter.

What systems would you use, and why, in the following situations:

(a) Your bank has arranged a loan for an import/export business. The loan agreement must be signed by both partners in the business, one of whom operates from and is domiciled in Jersey. The agreement needs to be signed in the next 24 hours.

(b) Your superior has been composing a report on his microprocessor. You have a short paragraph to add to the report on training of junior staff (this paragraph has already been approved). Your superior asks you to add your paragraph and then circulate it to all section heads immediately. Section heads will need it for discussion at a meeting the same day.

How will you accomplish this?

CONCLUSION

Since this chapter can only give a brief outline of some of the developments in communication technology and it is likely that your organisation already uses many of the systems mentioned, it is in your interests to find out as much as you can about them. Get to know how a system works and what facilities it provides for the conduct of financial transactions.

SUGGESTED ANSWERS TO ACTIVITIES

Activity 1

Advantages of the telephone:

(a) Accessibility — most people are subscribers. Service operates 24 hours a day.
(b) Convenience — easy to pick up the phone and dial to establish contact.
(c) Coverage — it is a world-wide network.
(d) Cost — it is relatively cheap.

Activity 3

Disadvantages of the telephone:

(a) Only fast and convenient if you can establish contact with the receiver.
(b) Businesses do not man their phones 24 hours a day.
(c) (a) and (b) may make telephone calls expensive in time and money.
(d) There is no permanent record of the transaction.

Activity 4

Ask your tutor to check this.

Activity 5

Year — 06 — 25 18:00

563289 NATEST G
456880 JENAT G

(Transaction number) Year — 06 — 25 18:00

Attn: P. Leblanc

Credit rating Ms J. Cottrell satisfactory

From: (insert own name)

563289 NATEST G
456880 JENAT G

Activity 7

(a) Fax would be the best method since you can get an exact copy of the agreement to Jersey. Public Fax can be used if the partner does not possess a Fax machine and the transaction can still be achieved within 24 hours.

(b) You could either use the local area network and electronic mail to send copies to section heads directly and they could produce their own printed copies. Alternatively you could use the LAN to send the edited report automatically to the intelligent copier for printing. The printed copies of the report could then be distributed.

ASSIGNMENT

Background Situation

You are working for six months in the International Department of your bank in London.

A hotel in Geneva is expecting a small delegation of three from your bank for an international banking conference. Arrangements had been made for them to arrive at the hotel on 5 March 19.. at approximately 5.00 p.m. There has been a change in their plans because they need to visit the branch of your bank in Geneva on 4 March to discuss changes in banking procedures. They will now need to be booked into the hotel from 9.30 a.m. on 4 March.

Tasks

It is 9.10 a.m. on 2 March and you have tried to telephone the hotel without success. You have checked and they have no telex facility. Consequently you have been asked to do the following:

(a) Draft a telegram for your superior to send to notify the hotel of the change in arrangements and to secure confirmation that they can accommodate the party of three for the extra day.

(b) Draft a telex message to be sent to the Geneva branch of your bank (the telex operator has the number) notifying them that the delegation will be arriving with them at approximately 11.00 a.m. and that the discussion is likely to continue into the afternoon. Senior staff at the branch should be available to participate in the discussion.

NB All times are given in British time. Make up appropriate names for the hotel, the bank and your superior.

PART 4

Communication within the Work Place

5 Note-taking, Note Form Summary/Précis

Whatever the task you may face in written and oral communication, an extremely useful skill is that of making precise and clear notes to summarise your thoughts or complex material. We have already discussed the importance of making notes in preparation for a telephone call or taking notes during one but the ability to make/take good notes has a wide variety of applications and is rightly valued by the banks in its employees and consequently it is tested in the training and qualifications they require.

Let's consider some of the areas in employment where good note-making can prove invaluable.

USES OF NOTE-MAKING/TAKING TECHNIQUES

ACTIVITY 1

Pause for Thought

Before we categorise where these skills may be useful, try to identify for yourself the tasks within your banking career for which notes may be essential and list these.

Generally, note-taking may be required in the following situations:

As Preparation *Before*

- Making a telephone call.
- Writing a letter.
- Composing a report.
- Attending a meeting or conference in which you are required to participate.

- Producing a summary of documentation, e.g. articles, policy documents, procedural changes, training notes—for other people's use.
- Producing a summary of oral material for others, e.g. reporting back from a training course, meeting, conference, etc.
- Interviews—selection, appraisal, discipline.

As a Recording Method

- Summarising the proceedings of both formal and informal meetings for your own use.
- Recording telephone messages for other people and for yourself.
- Recording, in summary form, written information for work purposes, e.g. summaries of articles relevant to your job.
- Condensing information drawn from a variety of sources relevant to one subject/topic.
- Recording information from interviews.
- Summarising information for an oral presentation at a meeting, training course, etc.

For Studying

- Aiding recall of oral or written information for study purposes.
- Condensing information drawn from a variety of source, e.g. books, articles, lectures.
- Concentrating listening skills.
- Assisting selection of relevant points while reading for comprehension and retention.
- Testing acquisition of information.

From these lists it is evident that effective note-making and note-taking techniques can assist our competence in much of the work which is characteristic of the banks. For this reason the relevant techniques are worth attention.

NOTE-TAKING

Note-taking while Reading

To some extent this is easier than taking notes when listening since the material can be reread as often as you wish. There are different ways of reading and we may not be aware that we do read differently for particular purposes. Some methods are:

- *Scanning* This normally involves looking for key words in reference books.

- *Skimming* This, on the other hand, means looking for the broad framework of ideas or facts within the material. It is here that subheadings can be invaluable in helping the reader to skim-read effectively. If there are no subheadings then it means identifying the key sentence(s) in each paragraph—often the first sentence. This is important when attempting to understand and record complex information or new procedures.

- *Reading for studying and critical reading* This is a much more concentrated activity and you will need to take notes not only to summarise but also to assess and evaluate what you read. By putting complex ideas in your own words you ensure your own concentration and the interpreting ensures that you really understand or comprehend the content.

  To do this adequately you may have to look up or check in some other way the meaning of vocabulary or content. It is only in this way that you expand your own knowledge and your own understanding of the business of banking.

  It is the reason for the inclusion of comprehension exercises in the qualifications demanded by the banks. All employees of the banks need, in any case, to update their knowledge and keep abreast of current trends, and banking periodicals and reviews as well as business supplements of quality newspapers are an extremely good source of such information.

Comprehension The Chartered Institute of Bankers examination rightly tests the ability to read and understand complex material. You are probably used to this kind of exercise from your full-time education studies but the material you are required to master here relates directly to the banking world. Passages set are drawn from a variety of sources such as bank reviews, periodicals, financial papers, etc. They all concern current trends in banking and finance but are of general, rather than technical interest.

It would be advisable to conduct a personal reading programme whereby at least one article on such a topic should be read for study purposes each month and due attention given to the vocabulary, arguments and ideas that it contains. A good dictionary is an essential aid in carrying out this practice and you might try note-taking in the schematic style (which we discuss later) at the same time.

The kinds of questions you are likely to be asked on such a passage are the meanings of certain words or phrases in the context of the passage and those which demand an ability to *identify important facts and arguments and to re-express these in your own words.*

Later in this chapter an activity/exercise is given which is primarily to practise note form summary techniques, but which also gives you some comprehension questions to try. The assignment for this chapter will also give further practice in these two activities.

Note-taking from Oral Material

This is more difficult since the information is quickly given and the speaker moves on. Nevertheless, any bank employee will be present, on occasions, when it is vital to record what has been said—at a meeting, interview, training course, etc. All that we have discussed concerning listening skills in Chapter 1 (page 16) is important here. You also need to develop the ability to select what is important and to omit what is merely digression, elaboration, repetition, example or illustration.

Whether you are dealing with written or oral material, the original note-taking is usually random—a collection of quickly jotted ideas and points. Unfortunately, when we read these later on or someone else tries to understand them, they are often incomprehensible; so it is important that immediately following the 'jotting' process, notes should be formalised and arranged under relevant subheadings which clarify the outline of the material.

ACTIVITY 2

Exercise

Record briefly the main points from a television or radio interview. As you watch/listen, take quick notes, attempting to select what is important only. Immediately following the interview attempt to formalise the notes in a logical sequence under subheadings.

Ask someone who has not seen the interview to read these to evaluate how much makes sense.

We have talked about formalised notes under subheadings as a technique which may assist your own comprehension and guide others not familiar with the original material. This is particularly useful, for example, if *you* have attended a meeting and have to inform others of the proceedings or if you have had access to written material and have to summarise it for others. The skill of organising notes in this way is usually known as producing systematic or *schematic notes.*

This layout can also be used to prepare notes for the composition of a written document, e.g. a report or the preparation of oral communication, e.g. addressing a meeting.

Schematic Notes

By this term we mean the organisation of notes into related groups of points which are numbered and subheaded clearly for present and future reference. For example, consider the passage below:

> The amount of paperwork produced by the banks indicates that most of the employees might well find it extremely difficult to complete all their tasks because of the volume of material they are expected to read, for example: instructions, rules, financial regulations, legal restrictions, economic constraints and the various pronouncements of the government of the day. In addition, they must compose a variety of communications which range from simple messages and instructions to letters and reports dealing with complex financial and personal problems. The awards of the Plain English Campaign have very rarely gone to the banks, which suggests they still have a long way to go towards writing clear and concise English.
>
> The conventions within banks concerning written communication have often led to unnecessary verbiage. 'Habits die hard' so the banks continue to produce documents which are difficult to understand, full of outdated jargon and lacking in diplomacy.
>
> The important principles are that: first, we choose the right word to produce the right result; second, clear communication saves money and time because it is more efficient for people to understand immediately what they hear and read without having to analyse it; third, people need to be able to understand information quickly to know their legal and financial rights and responsibilities.
>
> This argues a strong case for training bank employees in good communication techniques so that the public are not subjected to jargon. In the *Law Society Gazette* one writer identified some important points for lawyers that are equally true for bankers. These include: using everyday English, cutting out unnecessary phrases, avoiding technical language and avoiding, above all, long words and 'officialese'.
>
> The few simple rules, which are given here, help to achieve effective communication but, above all, we should think of the reader or the listener and write or speak for their purposes, not ours. Rudyard Kipling once said, 'Words are, of course, the most powerful drug used by mankind' so we have to make doubly sure that we use the right words to achieve the desired results.

In schematic notes this passage might be summarised as follows:

Effective Communication by the Banks

(1) *Present situation*

The volume of paperwork still creates difficulties for staff in understanding and composing communication.

(2) *Standards*

These are still considered poor.

Habits in outdated and tactless communication are still followed.

(3) *Principles of good communication*

These are:

(a) choice of correct word to produce desired result;
(b) it is more efficient and cost-saving to use immediately understandable language;
(c) public need to know and understand clearly their rights and responsibilities;
(d) omit unnecessary or complex words, technical/official language.

(4) *Need for training*

Effective communication is not difficult BUT does require awareness in bank employees.

This indicates need for bank training in good communication.

(5) *Conclusion*

Since words are both powerful and persuasive, you should choose those most suited to reader/listener.

You will note this is shorter than the original, avoiding repetition and examples; it gives clear subheadings to guide the reader, who can see the content of the whole passage at a glance. This is also the principle behind preparing the minutes of meetings (dealt with in Chapter 9).

It is worth noting here that there are a number of terms that apply to reducing original information to a shortened form. There is the *précis* which requires you to produce a shorter version of the original information, presented in continuous prose and retaining exactly the balance, features, layout and tone of the original.

Alternatively, you may be asked to produce an *abstract* which is a selection of material from a long piece of written information such as an article in a journal. You may be asked to write *minutes* which are a concise record of the proceedings and decisions at a formal meeting. However, the most likely form of presenting summarised information is the *note form summary*. For this reason it is tested in the examination. A précis may be required instead.

Note Form Summary

The note form summary required in the examination usually takes the form of reducing an article in a banking periodical from an original of some length. It is usually on a topical subject.

Techniques You should keep your objectives clearly in mind. These are: to summarise the original material but to include all the main points and to ensure it can be understood clearly by the reader. Use the following techniques:

(1) Read the passage through carefully to identify the subject, main facts, development of ideas.

(2) Write down a title which encapsulates the subject of the passage; you can use this later to check points for importance and relevance.

(3) Reread the passage identifying *topic sentences*; most paragraphs have a *topic sentence*—one which gives you the main subject of that paragraph. Generally no paragraph has more than three main points on this subject. (This is also discussed in Supplement 2, page 237). Use the topic sentences to decide on the subheadings for your summary. Underline the main points in each paragraph.

(4) Using your subheadings and your underlined points as guidelines, write out your summary. Ensure you have grouped related points together; it is a good idea to number your subheadings and the points beneath them (see example on page 102).

(5) Make sure that your information is presented consistently in terms of numbering, indentation, etc.

(6) Check back to ensure you have retained the *balance* of the original and not given undue weight to one section at the expense of another.

(7) (For examination purposes) Check the number of words in your summary, adjust as necessary and then write the total number of words at the bottom of your summary.

(8) Check back on basics such as spelling, punctuation, so that the summary is written in clear accurate English.

(9) Check back to your working title; ensure that the final title is brief and relevant. This should now appear at the top of your note form summary.

If you follow these rules, your summary should be a concise and precise record, presented in a form that the reader can understand. Remember that your final summary should make sense in its own right, i.e. without the reader having to refer to the original.

The Traditional Précis It is unlikely that you will be required to undertake this exercise in a work situation. However, some examinations still require this; it is important to *check* the examination question concerned to see which is required—a note form summary, or a précis.

The note form summary we have already discussed at some length. A *précis*, on the other hand, is a summary in *one continuous paragraph*. It is written in complete sentences and does *not* have subheadings or numbered points. It is also a requirement that you must write in your own words, without quoting directly from the original. Any direct speech or quotations in the original passage have to be paraphrased, and presented in an *indirect* form. Otherwise, points 1, 2, 6, 7, 8 and 9 given above still apply. (You should follow point 3 apart from deciding on subheadings.)

A final list of Do's and Don'ts which apply to *both* kinds of summary follows.

DON'T

- read superficially
- include points which are irrelevant, trivial or examples/illustrations
- copy whole sentences from the original
- make your summary a list of unconnected points

DO

- read the original carefully
- include key points
- ensure you maintain the sense, style and tone of the original
- produce a rough draft first so that you can edit it
- check the final version for errors in spelling, punctuation, and sentence construction

ACTIVITY 3

Exercise from a Specimen Paper: Note Form Summary and Comprehension

Even in this electronic age, few members of the public have much idea of the internal intricacies of the computer. Whilst most people are quite happy to live in blissful ignorance, this state of affairs presents a problem for the average bank manager.

The problem is that the growth industries in this country are technologically biased, and companies in those industries depend on banks for their financing. Bank managers will increasingly be called on to judge propositions involving high technology. A manager of a start-up electronics firm could be disillusioned by a bank manager's incomprehension and have difficulty in attracting funding.

The four major clearing banks each take a different approach to the situation: Lloyds and National Westminster have decided that a high-technology start-up should be considered as just another small business, whereas Barclays and Midland have both set up units within their corporate divisions, dealing exclusively with this sort of company.

Barclays claims to be a leader in the field, having established its high-technology unit in 1980. David Killick, the manager of the high-technology team, explains how the unit operates. 'Our team consists of technology specialists. We also use a lot of external consultants, like the Cranfield Institute of Technology and the National Engineering Laboratory at East Kilbride. There are also a number of people who will help the bank for no charge—we've *endowed* half-a-dozen different universities, for example, and we can always refer to them. Another major source of free technical advice is the Department of Trade and Industry (DTI).'

This technical expertise helps Barclays' managers to make decisions about the trading ability of a high-technology company, but as Killick says, technical merit is not the only consideration. 'The local branch manager will ask for a business plan, to be prepared along our guidelines. We find that a lot of these companies are managed by people who are technologically strong, but who are weak on the marketing side. The technical aspect is then of secondary importance. As long as the business plan meets *normal banking criteria*, with a management team of some *integrity*, there's an *acceptable capital structure*, and if the company already has debtors, then there is a firm basis to consider lending working capital.'

Although Killick stresses that the management team is more important than the product, he acknowledges that there has to be some assessment of its technical quality. 'The bank manager cannot make all the judgements. He or she would need to have some guidance on whether the product works, whether it would sell, and what the competition would be like. That, after all, is the reason the unit was set up.'

One invaluable source of expertise for project monitoring is the DTI's Joint Appraisal Scheme. Killick explains how the scheme works. 'We advise a company with a technically advanced product to apply for a grant. The case will be reviewed by scientists, who will then prepare a report. They can then provide us with the technical assessment that goes before the DTI's grant committee, at the same time asking us what we think of the *customer's financial acumen.*'

'If the company gets its grant, we can deduce that it was a strong technical report—that gives the bank more confidence in lending money. If a grant application is declined, even though the product appears to be excellent, it could be that there are applications for similar products in the pipeline.'

If the bank receives applications from companies with no trading record but an exciting product, Killick will be cautious. 'If the product was just an idea and there was no capital or business plan, we could be interested. In our experience, there is too much emphasis placed on the idea. An inventor might have a brilliant concept and considers that all the business associated with that idea will be easy. Marketing, pricing, documentation are all considered lesser skills. The bright idea is important but the other factors are equally important if that company is to be there in five years' time.'

The bank, however, will try to help companies with exiting products even if there are shortcomings on the business side. 'A manager will not feel able to lend working capital to any business organisation if normal banking criteria are not met', says Killick. 'But because we believe in high-technology companies as the way ahead for British industry, we may be able to introduce a company to *venture capitalists* or, possibly, introduce it to a larger organisation that could provide the financial stability to develop that product.'

This belief in the electronic and computer industry has prompted the bank to develop the technical expertise of their branch managers. 'We believe there is a degree of 'techno-fear' in bank managers generally. In order to combat this, we have organised awareness seminars for branch managers. They can learn how to handle circuit boards, listen to scientists and, we hope, gain a basic understanding of some of the technical terms used. Two-thirds of our managers have already attended these seminars. In due course, all our managers will have benefited from them.'

The bank, however, has organised further technological courses for a small selection of its managers, according to Killick. 'We run more in-depth courses, as we have decided to disseminate our technological expertise throughout the country. Consequently, we have established about 50 nominated "high-technology branches", starting in locations such as Reading and Cambridge, where the managers have undertaken this extra training. This ensures that individual branch managers will be able to talk to the technical people in their own language, and will be able to make decisions on a product's technical merit without recourse to the unit.'

Task

Summarise the above passage (note form summary) in not more than 250 words. In your own words give the meanings of the (following words and phrases used in the passage above):

endowed	line 22
normal banking criteria	line 31
integrity	line 32
acceptable capital structure	line 32
customer's financial acumen	line 46
venture capitalists	line 65

A suggested answer appears at the end of this chapter.

Note-taking is a means of summarising existing information. Note-making is usually a creative activity caused by the need to prepare an outline for a complex piece of oral or written communication. Note-making techniques will be considered next.

NOTE-MAKING

This technique will be necessary if you have to prepare a report, oral or written, present some information at a meeting or talk to a group. It is important, for example, in giving oral or written instructions, in composing letters and memoranda, in preparing for an interview. There are a number of techniques which may help you.

Techniques

(1) *Objectives* As with any communication, define your objectives and identify your readership/audience. This will influence what you will say or write, your choice of language and approach and the sequence of information you will use. These points need to be noted down in advance so that you can check your final draft for relevance.

(2) *Data collection* An essential area of preparation is to collect together all the necessary information, figures, illustrations, etc., relating to the subject to be treated or document to be composed. This is best done randomly at first—it can be sorted and organised at the next stage. Effective research is one of the most important steps in the compilation of notes.

(3) *Selection and sequence of information* Whenever you present facts or ideas in written or oral form it is easier for people to understand if the order is clear. You need to select the facts and ideas that are directly relevant to the topic and then group related facts and ideas together. You should

ruthlessly eliminate anything which is not relevant to your objectives or of interest to your readers/audience. Related points should be grouped under clear subheadings. You then need to decide on the correct sequence. The order should always start from the existing knowledge of the reader/audience and progress from there.

(4) *Subheadings and numbering for reference* Notes need to be headed and numbered logically so that you can refer to them quickly and easily. If you are talking from notes they will need to be written/printed in large letters so that they are easily legible and the subheadings emboldened, coloured or underlined so that you can refer to them at a glance. This will enable you to 'talk' to your audience maintaining good eye contact, rather than 'reading' your notes.

(5) *Annotation* Sometimes notes of this kind may need annotating, i.e. a comment shown in the margin against a point or a section. Annotation may be used to give, for example, a time allocation to deal with a particular subheading or a reminder to show a diagram at a particular point. More help will be given on the layout of notes for oral presentations in Chapter 8.

The important point to remember, once again, is that notes need to be clear and schematic.

Making Notes for Other People

Sometimes it is important that notes should be comprehensible to someone who is not present at a meeting, conference, exhibition, etc. In this case, effort should be made to present them as professionally as possible. They should be preceded by a clear title, a date and a reference as to why they were requested and by whom. It is more important than ever that the rules for note form summaries and those given above are followed. Some indication needs to be given as to whom should be contacted and how if any further information is required.

CONCLUSION

The ability to make and take good, clear concise notes which are immediately understandable, is an essential skill in a variety of situations you will encounter in your banking career and in your personal life. It is perhaps for this reason that the Institute has emphasised the need to develop these skills and assesses them in banking qualifications.

You might like to try one further exercise in conclusion.

ACTIVITY 4

Exercise

You have been with your bank for approximately nine months. As part of a recruitment campaign, your branch has asked you to be part of a delegation visiting local schools to give school-leavers a talk on working within a modern bank. Your part of the talk looks at the topic from the point of view of a junior employee.

Make notes for a *five-minute* talk on this topic.

Keep your notes as you will be needing them for an assignment in a later chapter.

SUGGESTED ANSWER TO ACTIVITY 3

Note Form Summary

Please note *schematic* approach with subheadings.

THE IMPACT OF COMPUTER TECHNOLOGY ON A BANK MANAGER'S WORK

1. *The Importance of Understanding Technology*

   (a) Few people understand computers fully, but bank managers today need to understand them in order to be able to judge propositions involving high technology.

   (b) Growth industries are concentrated in this area; they rely on the banks for finance, expecting managers to be familiar with their problems.

2. *The Major Banks' Policies*

   (a) Lloyds and Nat. West. treat such firms as normal small businesses.
   (b) Barclays and Midland have specialised units.

3. *Barclays Special Unit (Established 1980; Manager: D. Killick)*

   A field leader, this engages specialists, refers to expert consultants, and utilises its endowed universities and the Department of Trade and Industry (DTI) for free advice.

4. *Balancing Business and Technical Expertise*

   (a) The unit provides advice for bank managers on the technical quality and competitiveness of the product.

   (b) Bank managers must also make judgments about business acumen—bright ideas must be accompanied by sound business plans concerning capital and marketing.

   (c) Companies are often advised to apply for a grant from the DTI who give a free scientific appraisal of the product, helping the bank to assess financial feasibility.

   (d) Others with an exciting product, but little expertise, are recommended to use venture capitalists or a large company for development.

5. *Barclays Manager Training Courses*

   (a) ⅔ of managers have now attended familiarisation seminars.

   (b) 50 high-technology branches are being established where managers will receive in-depth training, eliminating their need to refer to the unit.

(239 words inc. title)

Comprehension Questions

(a) Endowed—means to support with funds; in this case the bank provides funds to support university courses, places or resources.

(b) Normal banking criteria—means the normal requirements or standards which a bank would need before giving its support.

(c) Integrity—means worthy of trust; by implication here it also means that such a management team would have acceptable credibility.

(d) Acceptable capital structure—means suitable methods to organise its capital correctly in terms of assets and liabilities.

(e) Customer's financial acumen—means the client's ability and shrewdness; his understanding of money matters.

(f) Venture capitalists—means those having capital to invest in new business which seems worth the risk.

ASSIGNMENTS

1 Note Form Summary

Your superior had been invited to attend a seminar on 'Career Development for Women in Banking' at the Bath Centre. She was unable to attend because of the pressure of work. An article has now been published concerning the seminar in 'Banking World'. She asks you to summarise this in brief note form for her with appropriate subheadings so that she can read it rapidly and understand the proceedings. Summarise the article which follows in not more than 250 words.

2 Reading for Comprehension

Using the article for the note form summary, answer the following questions:

(a) Explain the words underlined in your own words.

(b) For what reasons have there been changes in the 'male/female culture in the banking profession'? (paragraph 3).

(c) What is meant by the expression 'quality of life'? (paragraph 4).

CAREER DEVELOPMENT SEMINAR

BY ANGELA SHEEN

A joint Career Development Seminar under the auspices of the Bath Local Centre and the Wessex Group of Women in Banking was held in Bath on 12 November 1986

Thirty-nine delegates, consisting of thirty-seven females and two males spent the day discussing various aspects of career development and syndicates were led by professional management consultants on the topics – *Evaluating Personal/Professional Strengths and Weaknesses*; *Mapping out a Career/Life Plan*; *Removing Limits to our Success*; *Stress*; *How People Manage Home/Work Roles*.

The Wessex Group of Women in Banking had been anxious to hold such a seminar for some time, believing that there were numerous benefits. All banks in the area were approached for their support both by way of finance and leave of absence and it was most encouraging to find that all responded positively.

Colin Gale, president of the Bath Local Centre, chaired the proceedings, which were opened with a presentation by Martin Webber, regional personnel manager, Midland Bank, Bristol. He talked about the changing male/female culture in the banking profession which had been brought about by the need to maximise staff resources coupled with the effect of equal opportunities legislation. In the past, the attitudes of senior executives had inhibited women's progress, but selection was becoming more professional and objective. He confirmed that opportunities are there for women but that there is more demanding need for individuals to demonstrate their commitment both professionally and socially. NatWest was the first bank to hold 'women only' courses which have been recognised as an important aid in encouraging women to be more positive in their career attitude. Most of the other banks have followed the lead in this respect but in Midland it had been found that women often need to be persuaded to attend! Mr Webber felt that it was important for women in appointed and managerial roles to publicise themselves in order to encourage other members of staff. The banks fully recognise the benefits of becoming a member of Women in Banking and acknowledge the success of the organisation.

Following discussions in the syndicates, each group reported back in a plenary session. The main points to come out of the discussions were that it is important for individuals to identify their personal strengths and weaknesses and to build on their strengths by gaining technical knowledge and skills. Regular personal reviews were essential in planning a career/life plan. Limits should be defined, whether self-imposed or imposed by outside forces, and it is important to be realistic in one's aims and ambitions. Women often settle for mediocrity and suffer from guilt and torn loyalties, particularly when balancing career and family roles. There are difficulties in judging the effects of having children, both for males and females. However, we should not be concerned by the opinions of other people provided that we and our families are happy with our lives. Personal expectations can lead to stress and it is essential that a balance is struck between career and quality of life. We need to build in time for ourselves. We were asked to consider the statement "I promise never again to settle for less than absolutely everything". This brought some interesting reactions from the delegates! Some delegates were asked to spend two minutes talking about their personal attributes and achievements and this was found to be an extremely difficult exercise!

The final summing up was given by David Gammon, manager, Lloyds Bank, Bath. He said that the division between work and personal life is being eroded and individuals are looking more closely at their own needs. Organisations, including banks, have to meet the challenge of restructuring career paths and allowing more flexibility. The quality of life is important if individuals are to be effective. Banks may need to impose their wishes to meet organisational needs and more negotiations and better dialogue are essential. He also remarked that the banks were experiencing a shortage of skilled staff, yet the proportion of women in senior positions compared with the total percentage of female staff was negligible. Perhaps the wrong criteria are being used for selection!

Although the seminar was not intended to be women-orientated at the outset, the banks all regarded it as such. However, the two male delegates found it to be as useful and interesting to them as the female delegates. All matters discussed were relevant to both sexes. It was generally felt that further seminars should be held as there is a distinct advantage in bringing together staff of varying grades from each of the banks. This achieves wider discussions and would help to build a network of contacts. Staff of all the banks felt that there was a need for greater communication from head offices and welcomed the involvement of the senior management present.

The Wessex Group's programme of 1986/87 includes several 'workshop' sessions and talks by senior managers of different banks and it is expected that many of the delegates will follow up the seminar by attending some of these meetings.

The venture was an undoubted success and perhaps other local centres will consider organising similar events. □

Angela Sheen is Chairman of the Wessex branch of Women in Banking.

6 Effective Memoranda, Notices and Displays

The most common methods by which people communicate with one another within any work place, apart from talking face-to-face or by telephone, are by memorandum (memo), by putting up notices or by using other forms of visual display such as wall charts, graphs or diagrams. Probably the most frequently used day-to-day communication is the memo.

THE MEMORANDUM

The memo is the lifeblood of any organisation, including your own. Messages must be sent from one member to another giving instructions, requesting information, confirming arrangements and the memo is often used for these functions. They may be handwritten, on preprinted memo forms or in some organisations may be sent from workstation to workstation by electronic mail. Whatever form the memo may take in the future, it will remain an important form of communication in your work life.

The full title for the memo is the *memorandum* (memoranda in the plural) and, as the name suggests, its prime purpose is to jog the memory or act as a reminder to take action. It is a form of communication used *within* the organisation between employees. It is *never* sent to anyone who is not a member of the organisation, i.e. clients, customers, business associates.

Today the memo is used to fulfil a number of functions beyond mind jogging. The following table shows the wide variety of uses for the memo in a typical organisation.

Ways in which the Memo is Used in Organisations

Communicating DOWN the line of command	*Communicating UP the line* of command	*Communicating BETWEEN* departments or sections
Giving instructions	Responding to requests for information	Seeking help/ cooperation

Giving/requesting information	Making proposals	Giving/requesting information
Confirming arrangements	Confirming arrangements	Confirming arrangements
Praising/reprimanding	Explaining action	Negotiating agreement
Seeking cooperation	Seeking help	
	Making complaints	

As you can see the memo is used for virtually any communication purpose when it is important to have a permanent record of the message.

Common Faults in Memo Writing

You have probably received many memos in the course of your work. You may already be groaning as you remember some of those messages. Since the memo is in such frequent use it is also liable to frequent abuse!

ACTIVITY 1

Pause for Thought

It would be useful at this point to stop and think about some of the complaints you can make about memos you have received.

List the different kinds of faults you identify. Then check your list against those shown below.

Your list is probably quite long and identifies specific faults but it is likely to cover the following aspects:

- too many memos sent by some employees
- the memo is used when another form of communication would be preferable
- the memo is poorly laid out
- the style of the memo is wrong
- the memo does not contain sufficient/accurate information

Sometimes the sheer number of memos coming from one source causes us to miss the importance of individual messages. We mentally register, 'Oh, not another memo from . . .' and no longer concentrate on the actual contents. We probably relegate it to the pending tray, the filing or even the waste paper basket without much thought. Secondly, we may feel annoyed or upset that someone has used a memo rather than talking to us more personally. If we receive a memo which is poorly laid out, we are going to experience difficulty understanding and absorbing the information it contains. If the wrong style is used we may interpret the message in the wrong way because it has aroused a bad emotional response in us. Lastly, if the memo contains insufficient or, we suspect, inaccurate information then we have to waste time and effort chasing up that information.

These are the many ways in which memos can develop faults and this contributes to the countless numbers that are put aside unread, filed in pending trays, misunderstood and resented each year. If you can level any of the above complaints at other people in your organisation, then it is important that *you* do not develop bad habits. You must learn:

- when to use a memo
- how to design a memo
- what style to use

as well as ensuring that every memo you write fulfils the six C's of communication (see page 9).

Selecting the Memo

Despite its usefulness as a means of internal communication, you should not automatically reach for the memo pad whenever you want to send a message. There are many situations which are best handled in other ways.

ACTIVITY 2

Pause for Thought

Think very carefully how you would feel if you received *only* a memo in the following situations:

(a) You have put in a considerable amount of effort in recent weeks, including extra hours, to help your section get ready for the introduction of a new service for clients. Your boss sends you a brief memo to say 'thank you'.

(b) Your boss is changing methods of working within your section. This will involve you in following new and rather complicated procedures. He sends you a two-page memo to explain.

(c) Your top management announce to you that they are closing down your branch by a circular memo to all staff.

Admittedly the memo may eventually play some part in the above situations but initially most employees would prefer face-to-face contact. We like to hear good and bad news directly from the people concerned. It is more meaningful, we can judge its sincerity from facial expressions and, in the case of bad news, we like people to have the courage to face us with the news rather than hiding behind pieces of paper. In change situations we feel more secure if someone talks to us about the change so that we have a chance to express fears and have queries answered.

If you think carefully about situations in which you would prefer to receive a message by word of mouth (face-to-face or telephone) then you can begin to identify when you should not use the memo as the prime form of communication. Never hide behind a memo as a way of avoiding personal contact. If you are thinking carefully about when to use a memo, you will also avoid the first fault of writing too many. There are two simple guidelines for using the memo:

(a) to support some previous form of communication by acting as a reminder;
(b) to provide a permanent record of information.

Designing the Memo

Length The memo is a concise form of written communication, i.e. brief but to the point. You will find that most organisations will have two sizes of preprinted memo forms, A5 and A4. The A5 size is used for very short messages of four or five lines contained in a single paragraph. The A4 size is used for longer messages involving several paragraphs. If the information you need to provide takes up more than one side of A4, you need to select an alternative form of presentation, e.g. report. The mnemonic KISS is a useful reminder about length (see page 70).

Topic A memo should contain information relating to *one* topic only. Never try to combine messages on several topics in a single memo. It is a false economy!

ACTIVITY 3
Pause for Thought

Identify two reasons why it is unwise to combine more than one topic in a memo.

You will realise that the reasons you have noted down probably relate to:

- The receiver's ability to understand, absorb information and act on the message—we are selective in the attention we give to information and we prioritise. If more than one topic is included we run the risk of paying attention to and acting on the information in one part of the memo and ignoring the rest.

- Memos which are a permanent record must be filed. Where do you file a memo which covers several topics? You either become involved in elaborate cross-referencing and indexing or you have to take photocopies.

It is much wiser to keep to the principle of *one memo for each topic.*

Layout All memos, whether preprinted, electronic or handwritten need some basic information provided:

Type of information	*Heading used*
Who has written the memo name/job title	FROM:
Who is to receive the memo name(s) and job title(s)	TO:
When it was sent	DATE:
Any reference	REF:
What it is about	SUBJECT:

These headings are shown in the example on page 118.

If copies of the memo are to be sent to a large number of individuals, it may be necessary to attach a circulation list to the memo. When enclosures are sent with a memo this should be clearly identified by writing ENC: followed by a description of the enclosure (see example on page 118). The following should *never* be shown on a memo:

- a salutation, i.e. Dear Mr . . .
- a complimentary close, i.e. Yours faithfully

With typed memos it is normal for the writer to initial the memo at the end to indicate authenticity and to show that the memo has been checked for accuracy after typing.

Sequencing A memo should present information in a sequence that is easy and logical for the *reader* to understand. There should be:

- An introductory sentence/paragraph stating the purpose of the memo and enabling the reader to focus his/her attention on the topic.

- Main points set out in simple direct sentences and using numbered points wherever possible. Longer memos should be set out in clear paragraphs, each paragraph dealing with a specific aspect of the topic.

Example of memo layout

```
                  Name of organisation

                       MEMORANDUM

FROM: (name and position)          DATE:   (in full)

TO:   (name(s) and position(s))    REF:    (if relevant)

SUBJECT:  (topic heading)

Introductory sentence giving purpose, background information.

   1.  Numbered points giving information required.
   2.
   3.

Concluding sentence defining action required of receiver.

                                   (initials of sender)



ENC.  (description of enclosure(s))
```

- A concluding sentence/paragraph identifying what the reader needs to do about the information and when.

Choosing your Style

While good layout is one important element in enabling the reader to understand and act on the message, another factor which you must consider is style. Style covers your use of sentence construction, vocabulary and tone and you need to adapt the style of a memo according to each situation. The factors which influence style are shown in the table below.

Factors determining the style to be used in memo writing

Receivers	superiors subordinates people on same level of authority people in same specialised section people in other parts of the organisation

Message	information giving information seeking persuading reprimanding praising
Immediate situation	routine crisis positive negative
Organisational style	formal informal autocratic democratic
Action needed	simple complicated routine new critical

Selecting the right style can produce a positive reaction in your reader but selecting the wrong style can lead to feelings of insult, anger, resentment and hurt. Such reactions are not likely to help you achieve your purpose.

Let's look at one example and analyse the suitability of the style in relation to the factors shown in the table.

> Thanks for the info. on the Parker file. I'll burn the midnight oil and let you have answers to your queries tomorrow—say 10.30 a.m.! Is that OK?

This memo acknowledges the receipt of information from another person, indicates that the writer will spend time and effort examining the contents and will answer the reader's queries at approximately 10.30 tomorrow. It invites a response from the reader to confirm that the arrangements are acceptable. The style is casual, friendly and uses abbreviations and familiar phrases.

It would not be appropriate to use this style:

(a) to many superiors (unless they have indicated they support a casual approach from subordinates);

(b) to people outside your own specialist area (unless they are very familiar with the Parker file and you *know* they favour an informal approach);

(c) to someone who is not familiar with well known phrases in the English language (who may be confused about what you mean);

(d) in an organisation that favours an autocratic style of management, (this would be seen as being too familiar with other members of the organisation and could undermine authority);

(e) in an organisation that is formalistic in its communication, (this would be seen as casual, imprecise and sloppy);

(f) if there had been no previous conversation or correspondence about the Parker file (the memo is too vague and is open to misinterpretation).

It would be appropriate if the memo is a friendly acknowledgement of receipt of information and a reminder of the action you agreed to take, written to a colleague in the same specialism or a boss with whom you have a close working relationship and who encourages a casual approach. It would only be appropriate if you had discussed the Parker file previously with the reader and both of you had agreed exactly what action was required. Even so, it would only be acceptable as a form of communication in an organisation which sanctioned an informal approach. If a more formal style is required, you could write:

> I have received all the information relating to the Parker file, ref. PA 147. I shall carry out a thorough analysis of the information within the next twenty-four hours and will then be able to answer your queries. Can we meet at 10.30 a.m. tomorrow to discuss the file?

MESSAGES BY E-MAIL

Today, many organisations are using E-mail (see Chapter 4 page 91) for sending internal messages. Some internal E-mail packages provide a template for messages so that entries can be keyed in against displayed prompts. This makes layout easy. Electronic messages have affected the style of memo writing. E-mail can often be used to replace the spoken word on the telephone and, on these occasions, uses the same type of spoken language, e.g. "Ok. Got your message. Will get back to you by 11.30 a.m. Bye." These are the types of message that can be wiped off memory after a few minutes. However, do not lapse into this style for all E-mail messages. You still need to adapt the style to the content, receiver and situation.

The ease with which messages are sent by E-mail can also be a disadvantage. Since it is so quick and easy, it is possible to send a message composed hurriedly which you might regret later. Memos dictated to a typist, typed up and then checked allow time to reconsider — you can correct an over-familiar or rather aggressive style and eliminate jargon. Always give the same consideration to your screen-composed messages before committing them to the E-mail out-tray!

It is important to remember that although memos are used frequently and therefore people are accustomed to writing a number of them daily, they nevertheless require considerable care in layout, composition and style if they are to be fully understood and if they are to encourage the right response. The principles which have been described should help to achieve this objective. The check-list below reminds you of them:

DON'T

- send a memo to people outside the organisation
- bombard people with too many memos
- use a memo just to avoid personal contact
- write sloppy memos with poor layout or style
- cover more than one topic in a memo

DO

- think about the receiver(s) before you write
- use a logical sequence for the information
- remember KISS (see page 70)
- consider all the factors which determine appropriate style
- remember the 6 C's (see page 9)
- check that the desired action has been carried out

If memos need careful composition, it is even more essential in the case of the notice.

NOTICES

Notices, like memos, suffer from the limitations of being one-way communication; you have no idea whether they have remained unread, their message ignored or whether they have aroused resentment which you did not foresee. Therefore you need to take care with their composition, layout and their position.

Some people also fail to discriminate between when you should use a memo and when you should use a notice. They are not necessarily interchangeable.

Function of the Notice

Notices should only be used when there is a need for *mass communication* and where the message it contains is either important to everyone in the organisation (as in the case of safety) or is a matter of selective interest only (for example, giving notice of a social event) which people will either want to read or not. Notices should only be used if the *message also lends itself to visual display* techniques. Yellowing notices of typewritten paper which have remained unread for months are only too common. Notices should not be used where the message is specific to a small number of identifiable people and/or is sufficiently vital to require that everyone who is concerned has received it individually.

There are some documents which are displayed on notice-boards which are not strictly notices at all. They are reference documents which have often been sent to everyone but need to be displayed, too, e.g. lists of extension numbers, organisation charts, travel allowances. These, although they need to be displayed, are not covered by the principles discussed below.

Composition of the Notice

Basic principles are more often neglected in notices than in other methods of communication. Because they attempt to be brief they are often abrupt, if not arrogant, and they can therefore arouse responses which are not only indifferent but even resentful. Consider the following:

JUNIOR BANK PERSONNEL *MUST* NOT PARK THEIR VEHICLES IN THE PARKING BAYS MARKED A—F.

Signed: ....

ACTIVITY 4
Pause for Thought

What is wrong with the above notice?

See if you can list three points before reading on.

The notice shows very little understanding of human reaction; it certainly does not give any attention to an important communication objective—obtaining the right response. You may have noted the following points:

- The notice begins by discriminating against a particular group of employees and is thus liable to produce a rebellious response—Why us? Many will probably try parking in these bays to see what happens.
- It is a direct order which is abrupt and very autocratic—nobody responds well to this approach.
- As the notice gives no reason why people should not park in these bays, it poses a challenge.

The net result is that people will be compelled by a combination of curiosity and anger to have a go—not precisely the response required!

ACTIVITY 5
Exercise

Think of a legitimate reason for the instruction quoted in the notice above. Then recompose the notice.

A suggested answer appears at the end of the chapter.

Display

Location of the notice Notices should be located either in direct proximity to where they are relevant, e.g. 'Please switch off the lights' above the light switch, or in a well-lit central position which everyone passes daily and where they have time to linger, e.g. by the coffee machine, in the cloakroom, by the lockers.

Initial attraction Because a notice may remain unread unless it attracts attention it is important to employ all the techniques you can to attract attention.

Wording One desperate person composed his notice as follows:

S E X !

> Now I've attracted your attention I have the following car for sale:
>
> ....

It is not, of course, advisable on a formal notice-board to go to this extreme, but the message should be clear.

The following are important in attracting attention before you begin the main message otherwise it will not get read at all—particularly on an overcrowded, outdated notice-board which has not been read for some time:

- size of letters
- heading of the notice
- the first phrase
- the initial stimulus, whatever it may be

To avoid an overcrowded notice-board someone should always be made responsible in an organisation/department for clearing outdated notices from boards, otherwise they are never removed—we all pass the buck.

Colour of pictures/printing Coloured paper, colour pens, large lettering and underlining all help to attract and maintain the eye of the passer-by. Small typewritten notices do not. Some notices also lend themselves to pictorial devices, e.g. health and safety notices designed to shock, themes for social events. Of course, there are some notices which are so formal that they must appear in a fairly conventional form—these are normally those composed by higher management and since communication is a two-way process, it is important that you do your duty as a receiver and read them—however boring!

One exception to all rules is a notice of a meeting which, by its nature, is nearer to a memo and is discussed in the chapter on meetings. Normally, however, the important thing to remember is that notices should combine the principles of effective communication with the techniques of effective display.

OTHER FORMS OF VISUAL DISPLAY AT WORK

There are a number of other forms of visual display which are employed within work organisations. These include:

- *Planning charts*—for events, holiday rotas, necessary work deadlines. Provided these are kept up-to-date and the entries are made in large letters/numbers/symbols, they are an excellent aid to time management and have instant impact on everyone in the work area. They also need to be well designed, to give adequate space to relevant entries, so choosing one that is appropriate to your special needs is important.

- *Bar charts, line graphs, diagrams, etc.* These are most often used to present figures in an easily assimilated form and are as important for internal communication as they are for informing customers.

- *Visual display units* Another way of displaying data to a number of people is to show information graphically on the VDU of a microcomputer or computer terminal. Charts, graphs and diagrams can be available for immediate access and information can be distributed in this form by electronic mail (see Chapter 4).

Holiday Planner *Key* O

Name	January					February				March				April					May				June			
	1	8	15	22	29	0	13	20	27	6	13	20	27	3	10	17	24	31	7	14	21	28	4	11	18	25
J. SMITH																O	O									
T. CHANG	O	O																								
G. HOLMES																										
P. HARRIS																					O	O				
C. SALMON																										
P. WEBSTER																									O	O

Planning charts

CONCLUSION

As this chapter has shown, there are several methods which are available for communicating between people within the work place. The major principle involved is to choose carefully which method is appropriate in the light of:

(a) what is to be conveyed;
(b) why the message is needed;
(c) to whom it is addressed.

Choosing should be a conscious and careful process and *always* take into account these factors.

Although these are routine methods of communication they should never be treated lightly if they are to be effective and are to gain the required response.

SUGGESTED ANSWER TO ACTIVITY 5

SHORT-TERM CAR PARKING SPACES

The bays marked A—F have been reserved for short-term visitors from Head Office and other branches. They may also be used by specific members of this branch who are required to travel on bank business daily and who have been issued with CREAM PERMITS to display on their windscreens.

Other staff are therefore requested to leave
these spaces free.

You may feel that such a notice should be reinforced by individual memos to ensure that the message was read by everyone. If so, well done! There is no harm in using two methods of communication rather than one.

ASSIGNMENT

Your bank is keen to encourage contact between young employees within the region through combined social activities. One of the events aimed at this purpose is the annual May Day dance. Each year a different branch organises this and plans the activities. This year it is the turn of your branch and the Assistant Manager has asked you, as representative of the newer employees, to coordinate this project.

(a) As your first task you decide to send a *memo* to all your colleagues in the branch asking for ideas about suitable activities; (you should suggest some of these to give them some initial examples). You also want to ask for volunteers to help you plan and organise the event.

Task

Compose a suitable memo to gain the response you need.

(b) Assume you have received all the replies to your memo and a number of suitable activities have been suggested (you can invent for yourself what these might be). A number of people have volunteered to help and the planning is now well ahead. You have decided on a suitable location, have hired the musical and catering facilities required and have decided on the costs of the tickets to cover expenditure and make a small profit to provide raffle and other prizes.

You are now ready to design a *notice* to be displayed in all the region's branches. Naturally you want to sell as many tickets as possible.

Task

Design the required notice using relevant display techniques.

7 Report Writing

THE NEED FOR CLEAR REPORT WRITING

One of the most important and complex documents you may be required to produce is the report. It is here that good note-making techniques can be extremely helpful in the preparation stage. Clear and accurate reports are crucial if information is to reach those who need it to make decisions; they should be as brief as possible, yet contain all the facts which the reader needs. This is actually quite difficult to achieve, and there has been considerable criticism of report writing standards from employers. It is for this reason that the banks place emphasis on the need to develop good report writing skills.

ACTIVITY 1

Pause for Thought

What reports have you read to date? What was their purpose? How were they laid out? How successful were they in conveying exact information to the reader quickly and easily?

You may have thought immediately of school reports. Their purpose was twofold—to record your achievement and progress for the reference of the teaching staff and yourself, and to convey information to your family and other interested parties. They may well have been used when you entered employment as the basis for a reference.

Usually, they are laid out as a standard form, with columns for examination and course-work grades, teachers' comments, etc. They need to be regularly given and to be filled in by a number of people fairly quickly, so a form layout is appropriate here.

How well they convey exact information, however, will be related directly to the skills and efforts exhibited by the individual teacher, or will be determined by how clearly the purpose of the report is defined for them. 'Fair, but could do better' does not actually give precise facts to the reader. Other entries may be far more accurate, giving detailed comments on the strengths and/or weaknesses of the individual. Clearly this is far more useful if the report is to be used for later references and for the student to attempt to improve his/her performance.

At work, a similar function is performed by assessment or appraisal reports, which you may have seen too; these are also laid out as a form and they contain specific questions to be answered or performance standards to be assessed.

Usually there are two parts to the form, one for the individual employee to complete and one for his/her immediate superior, so that both can identify the strengths and weaknesses in performance.

Again, these are used as a record of progress and often contain information related to training needs, future potential for promotion or even salary level. Therefore, they need to be precise and accurate. The example on page 129 helps us to identify what a report should aim to achieve.

THE PURPOSE OF REPORTS

We can see that reports have two aims:

- To give adequate and accurate information to the reader; to fulfil this aim the report should be concise but sufficiently comprehensive for the reader to make informed decisions.
- To record information for later reference; it must therefore be presented briefly and in a logical format.

Simple Reports: The Routine Report on a Form

Reports on forms such as the one we have identified earlier can assist here. You may have thought of many others—accident or safety report forms for instance. You may even have had to fill in one of these—perhaps not for the bank but for the police or an insurance company.

Certainly, the first reports which you may have to compose will probably be of this type. They are relatively easy to prepare, because the form itself indicates what should be there—always supposing that it is well designed!

ACTIVITY 2
Exercise

Collect examples of reports on forms used by your own organisation. These might include annual assessment report forms, accident forms, etc. How easy/difficult would you find them to fill in? Do they contain the right questions/sections to provide all the information necessary? You might like to compare these with examples from other organisations. One example of a routine report is given on pages 129–131.

However well a form is designed to obtain the information needed, the usefulness of what it contains will depend very much on the effort and ability of the person compiling the report to give accurate and complete information which is directly relevant to the form's purpose. If you have to complete this type of report you should always bear in mind who will be reading the information and

Appraisal form – Example of a routine report

NAME ....

Position held in Bank ....

Name of Branch ....

Department ....Age ....

Length of Service ....

STAFF APPRAISAL FORM

The objectives of an Appraisal Form are:—

1. To aid selection of staff for promotion
2. To decide the development required for the employee
3. To meet industrial relations requirements
4. Basis for salary review

Broadly, an appraisal should establish:—

1. If an employee has been told his job
2. If an employee has been given the skills to perform his job
3. If an employee has been given the tools to perform his job
4. If an employee has been given the authority to perform his job

	Ratings*	Comments
Appearance		
General Conduct and Relationship with Colleagues and Customers		
Timekeeping		
Accuracy of Work		
Knowledge of Procedures		
Communication		
Ability to accept Responsibility		
Delegation (where applicable)		
Development and Motivation of Staff (where applicable)		
Quantity of Work		
Quality of Work		
TOTAL	______	
AVERAGE	______	

*Rating

100—96 Excellent — an outstanding performance obvious to all

95—91 More than satisfactory

90—86 Satisfactory—is performing the job for which employed

85—81 In need of improvement

80—76 Not acceptable — possibly a new appointment into the job

What are your strengths?

What are your weaknesses?

How can the Bank or your superior help you to improve your job performance?

Action	Time

What do you hope to achieve within the Bank?

When do you hope to achieve your objectives?

Promotion Potential:

I agree/disagree* with the foregoing comments

Appraisee ....

Appraiser .... Date ....

*I disagree with the following:

how it will be used. If you keep the purpose of the report clearly in mind this should help you to provide the right information even if the report form itself is poorly designed.

This ability becomes even more important when there is no form to assist you, as in other types of report. There are more complex kinds of report for which a form will not be appropriate since the composition of the information required is not of a routine nature and cannot be fitted into a predesigned form. It is here that you may need more guidance on the preparation, layout and style which are required. Although such reports may fulfil many different specific objectives, they fall into two categories for report writing:

(a) the information report;
(b) the investigation report.

Information Reports

As the name implies, this kind of report exists to *inform* others; it should do this by giving a brief subheaded summary of the matter to be communicated. For this kind of report this may be relevant facts concerning a training course, conference or exhibition you have attended, a brief written version of financial data, or an outline of material you have researched for the benefit of other interested parties. Since many information reports are, in fact, summaries of longer or more complex material you should refer back to the section on summaries in Chapter 5, page 103.

Investigation Reports

This goes beyond the simple information-giving process. It records the investigation of a problem/situation or a proposal for change. It may, for example, investigate whether a change in procedures might cut costs or add to efficiency, it may investigate new possibilities in working patterns such as flexi-time, or a reorganisation of the branch layout. Usually therefore it will require some recommendations or proposals for future action at the end for the consideration of whoever requested the report.

The layout and structure of these two types of report are slightly different but the initial preparation stage for both follows the same principles.

ACTIVITY 3
Pause for Thought

There are a number of forms in use in your branch which are causing difficulties. A report is to be compiled analysing these and suggesting possible improvements. Assuming you have been asked to help with this report, what information would you need and what methods would you use to collect such information?

PREPARATION OF REPORTS

You may have thought of:

- ▶ collecting examples of the forms
- ▶ interviewing members of staff and/or the public for their views
- ▶ analysing the forms in relation to the comments made

However, did you think of checking those things which affect the report writing itself, i.e.:

- ▶ the exact purpose of the report
- ▶ the date when it is required
- ▶ whether *you* are required to give any recommendations or not
- ▶ who will be reading the report?

You can only begin to select *relevant* information and conduct your investigation using appropriate methods if you know the answers to the above points. A checklist for the preparation and planning of both information and investigation reports is given below:

(1) Have I established clearly the aims and purpose of the report, its type and its exact requirements?

(2) Am I clear what the reader wants to know and why?

(3) Am I clear as to the limitations imposed on my preparation in terms of time and money?

(4) Am I clear as to what resources are available to me in terms of published material, records?

(5) Are other methods available for gathering information, such as observation accompanied by notes (as in the case of an information report) or interviews, discussions, questionnaires (as in the case of an investigation report)?

(6) When all the necessary information has been gathered, do I now have some facts and ideas which are irrelevant to the reader's needs and which can be eliminated?

(7) Of the remaining facts and ideas, which relate to one another and can be grouped in the final report?

(8) What subheadings might be suitable for these groups of related facts which will guide the reader and act as a reference point if the reader wishes to select a part of the report for consideration?

(9) What sequence of information is most logical for the reader to understand?

(10) Have I checked that I have not omitted anything that the reader needs to know?

STRUCTURE

Although the preparation stage for either kind of report contains the same processes covered by the ten points above, the structure differs slightly according to whether it is a report for information only or records an investigation.

Information Report

Depending on the length needed the information report may appear on a memo form, or it may appear as a separate document in its own right complete with title page. The main sections which dictate the content and layout, however, will remain the same, and they are as follows:

(1) *Introduction* (sometimes known as Terms of Reference)

This gives:

(a) the purpose and subject of the report;
(b) the name/position of the person(s) who requested the report and the date for submission;
(c) the name/position of the person(s) compiling the report;
(d) any necessary background information as to sources of information, dates/location of a visit/conference, etc.

(2) *Information* (sometimes referred to as Analysis of Information)

This section will give in *schematic* layout and with a logical sequence the major points or facts which are essential to the reader's interests and knowledge.

It will be further subheaded according to the kind of information it contains, and under each subhead will appear numbered points. This signposting is essential both to guide the reader through the material and, because the report is a reference document often used for discussion, so that the reader may select one section quickly.

(3) *Conclusion*

This should briefly summarise the main points which are priorities for the attention of the reader or for future consideration. Sometimes it is also required to give an *evaluation*—for example, of a training course—to assist others to make decisions.

(4) Signature and date—reports should always be signed and dated, or in the case of a report in memo layout, initialled.

An example of a short information report appears on pages 136–137.

If an information report is very long and complex (and you are unlikely to be asked to compile such a report at this stage in your career although you may receive one to read) it may also contain:

(a) a contents page;
(b) a list of illustrations and diagrams;
(c) a number of appendices containing extra information;
(d) a bibliography listing all the published material;
(e) a list of acknowledgements to other sources of information.

On pages 138–139, there appears another example of an information report—this time, on a memo form. This would be used for an internal report and you are likely to be asked to compile short reports of this type at this stage in your career. Although it follows the same sequence and structure as the previous example, the main headings—Introduction, Information and Conclusion—are omitted because with a report of this length they are not really necessary.

Information reports are frequently required quite early in a business career; once the principles and layout discussed here have been followed they are fairly straightforward in terms both of preparation and composition. The most complex type of report, and one which you may not be required to write until later in your career, is the *investigation report*.

Example of an information report

REPORT ON ONE-DAY TRAINING COURSE FOR JUNIOR CLERKS

IN CUSTOMER RELATIONS

1. INTRODUCTION

Two junior clerks from the Ockingham Branch attended the above course at Head Office on Tuesday 12 March 19... They were asked to compile a report on this and to submit it to the Assistant Branch Manager by 18 March 19... The purpose of the report was to provide information concerning the course for junior employees.

2. ANALYSIS OF INFORMATION

2.1 Content

The course was divided into three sessions:

2.1.1 Customer relations conducted by letter: 2 hours.
2.1.2 Customer relations conducted by telephone: 2 hours.
2.1.3 Face-to-face encounters with customers: 3 hours.

2.2 Training methods

2.2.1 Letters to customers
- The layout and style of letters required by the Bank was discussed by the Training Officer and a guidance hand-out was supplied.
- Examples of customers' letters to the Bank which requested information or complained about poor service were studied by course members in pairs and answers were prepared.
- These were then compared within the group with reference to layout, style, approach and diplomacy, and some general principles were drawn up on the flip-chart.

2.2.2 Telephone communication with customers
- A training video was shown which demonstrated the right and wrong ways of behaving on the telephone.
- Trainees were then divided into pairs and given roles, one as a customer, one as a

bank employee. Practice calls were then carried out, recorded and played back to the whole group. These were discussed and some general principles recorded.

2.2.3 Face-to-face encounters with customers

- A lecture was given by the Training Officer on the major problems and how to deal with them.
- A video was shown illustrating methods of dealing with typical customer problems.
- The trainees were again divided into pairs and given roles; the encounters were filmed, played back to the whole group and discussed. Some general principles were recorded.

3. CONCLUSIONS

The clerks who attended from this branch agreed that the course was worth while; it gave useful practice in handling situations which they have to face. This was very valuable as a preparation for communicating with customers diplomatically. It was also interesting to share experience and knowledge with trainees from other branches.

Signed......................

File: EXINRPT.001

Example of an information report on a memo form

MEMORANDUM

FROM: Miss P.L. Barnes
Senior Clerk

TO: R.P. Mann
Assistant Manager

DATE: 10 August 19..

SUBJECT: Training in the use of microcomputers for junior staff

In answer to your request of 5 August 19.. for a report by today's date I have enquired about courses available in the local area which might be suitable for junior staff at this branch; information is also given on transport and costs.

<u>Courses available:</u>

(a) Ockingham College of Further Education
1 day a week beginning 1 October 19..
duration - 12 weeks
cost - £80
distance - ½ mile from branch; bus service frequent.

(b) Worth College of Technology
2 evenings a week beginning 27 September 19..
duration - 10 weeks
cost - £75
distance - 5 miles from branch; bus service frequent.

(c) Skillscentre, Whitworth Road, Ockingham
3 weeks short course beginning 1 September 19..
cost - grants available - to be negotiated with Skillscentre
distance - ½ mile, no bus service.

Additional information:

(a) Some staff will still be on holiday on 1 September.
(b) The Skillscentre course would require a number of staff to be absent for long periods.

Courses (a) and (b) are the most feasible, and the costs involved are comparable.

I hope that this report provides enough information for you to make a satisfactory decision.

Investigation Report

As stated earlier, this is a document which records an investigation into a problem, incident or situation; usually, it involves a proposal for change in the future. It is therefore necessary at the preparation stage to give considerable thought to the kinds of investigation *methods* open to you, and what would be most appropriate related to the problem that faces you. The report also needs to include a record of these methods and to give proposals or recommendations.

The layout, therefore, will differ slightly from that of a report which summarises information only. The structure normally contains *five* major sections:

(1) *Terms of Reference*

This section will give all the information which has been listed in the information report (page 134) under (1)(a)—(c). It will also state whether recommendations are required.

It will *not*, however, include the sources/methods used to gather the data required, since these are likely to be more numerous and/or complex than those required for an information report. These methods of investigation warrant a separate section, as follows:

(2) *Methods of Investigation* or *Methodology*

This section lists the number of sources of information (e.g. files or textbooks) or methods of investigation (e.g. interviews, questionnaires) which you have used to gather your information. A number of these have been discussed earlier on pages 133–134. You might like to check back here, or even use them as a check-list when you have to write a report to see whether you have considered all the methods you might use and whether you have chosen methods appropriate to the subject of your investigation.

The methods section is important, for it shows the reader that you have thought carefully and investigated conscientiously. It leads logically to the next section which summarises the information which you have gathered from each source listed.

(3) *Findings* or *Analysis of Information*

As in the information report, this constitutes the major section; it contains the main facts and ideas grouped together in a logical way under subheadings and numbered points. These subheadings should be appropriate to the material, guiding the reader through the main section and providing an immediate outline for reference purposes.

Attention should be given to the most logical sequence. Sometimes subheads can refer back to the methods section. For example, if one of your methods was interviewing staff, then one of your subheads in the findings section may be 'staff interviews'. This is helpful to the reader who wants to see the exact source of the information.

Sometimes, a structure may suggest itself. For example, if you are discussing two possible new procedures, either of which could be recommended for adoption, the subheadings will almost automatically divide the information into:

Proposal 1

(a) Advantages
(b) Disadvantages

Proposal 2

(a) Advantages
(b) Disadvantages

The important principle is that the structure should help to signpost the reader through the material.

(4) *Conclusions*

As in the information report the conclusions section summarises the priority matters for attention and offers some evaluation of these; it should always be *shorter* than the findings section. It should lead logically to:

(5) *Recommendations*

This section lists the recommendations or proposals for future action for the consideration of the person/people who requested the report. They are, therefore, only *advisory*—the decision will still be taken by the reader.

Nevertheless, they are important and influential factors in affecting future action and decision-making, so sufficient and careful thought should be given to them. Often, costs which may have appeared in the 'Findings' section are reiterated here against the proposals to which they relate, so that the reader can be reminded of them and refer to them quickly.

Remember, finally, that no *new* material should ever appear in sections 4 and 5—the recommendations should be seen as a clear and logical outcome from the findings and conclusions.

An example of an investigation report appears on pages 142–143.

Example of an investigation report

REPORT ON SUPPORT FOR A SOCIAL CLUB FOR JUNIOR EMPLOYEES

1. TERMS OF REFERENCE

The Ockingham Branch of National Eastern Bank PLC have recently moved to new and larger premises. A room is available for social purposes and the Branch Manager has requested J.E. Brown, clerk, to investigate the views of the junior staff as to the activities which might be provided. The report is to be submitted by 15 March 19.. giving recommendations.

2. METHODS OF INVESTIGATION

2.1 The room was surveyed.
2.2 Junior staff were interviewed.
2.3 Cost and legal implications were investigated.

3. FINDINGS/ANALYSIS OF INFORMATION

3.1 Room survey

The room measured 30' x 17'; it has 2 large windows, 2 doors, is fully carpeted and has ample power points.

3.2 Interviews

The junior staff interviewed expressed the following preferences about facilities and activities:

3.2.1 a half-size snooker table should be provided;
3.2.2 table tennis equipment should be purchased;
3.2.3 a darts board should be installed;
3.2.4 bar facilities would be welcomed;
3.2.5 employees would be willing to pay a small fee to become members.

3.3 Costs and legal implications

3.3.1 In terms of costs:
- prices were investigated concerning the above facilities and are listed in Appendix 1;
- a fee of about £10.00 per head per annum would be sufficient for the initial year; the fee could be reviewed annually.

3.3.2 In terms of legal implication:
- a bar licence would need to be negotiated with local magistrates; regulations are listed in Appendix 2.

4. CONCLUSIONS

The room is suitable and most young staff would welcome a social club; they would be willing to pay to implement their suggestions.

5. RECOMMENDATIONS

It is recommended that the Branch Manager should consider:

5.1 that the room should be allocated to the staff social club;
5.2 that an initial fee of £10.00 should be charged for the first year;
5.3 that the suggestions should be implemented as soon as possible, taking into account costs and legal implications.

Signed...................

File: EXINVRPT, 001

OTHER POINTS ON LAYOUT

Numbering

There are a variety of ways in which the sections and subsections of a report may be numbered. Usually there is a house style—that is, your particular bank prefers one system—so you will need to check on this. Two possible systems are shown below:

Example 1	*Example 2*
I INTRODUCTION	1. INTRODUCTION
1.	1.1
(a)	1.1.1
(b)	1.1.2
2.	1.2
(a)	1.2.1
(b)	1.2.2
II ANALYSIS OF INFORMATION	2. ANALYSIS OF INFORMATION
1.	2.1
(a)	2.1.1
(b)	2.1.2
2.	2.2
(a)	2.2.1
(b)	2.2.2

The second of these, because it is more exact, is often preferred, but you can probably see from the example that where a number of subsections are required the digits can become rather numerous and confusing. If your bank prefers this style, therefore, you need to be particularly careful that each number is absolutely accurate. The important principles are that:

- ▶ numbering must *be accurate*
- ▶ numbering must *be consistent*
- ▶ numbering must be *clear to the reader*

so that the reader can refer quickly to the section required.

The Appendix or Appendices

Occasionally, you may have to compile a report which requires a set of diagrams, or a map or a set of statistics. Usually these appear at the *end* of the report as an appendix. If there is more than one appendix, you will need to number the appendices so that you can refer to the relevant one in the text of the report when this is required (i.e. see appendix . . .). Usually appendices are only required in longer reports, which you are likely to encounter later in your career, but even with a short report, it may sometimes be necessary to include one.

The Bibliography and/or List of Acknowledgements

If you have used a number of sources or consulted a number of people during the preparation of your report it is usual to list the sources and acknowledge the help of those concerned, at the end of your report. A list of published sources is usually referred to as a 'Bibliography', whereas those who have been consulted usually appear under the heading 'Acknowledgements'; the list is introduced by a phrase such as, 'The author of the report would like to thank those listed below for their help:'.

The Synopsis or Summary

If a report is very long—and you are unlikely at this stage to have to prepare such a document—a summary or synopsis of the main findings and recommendations is often attached to the *front* of the report, giving the whole outline at a glance. This is because such reports are often circulated to a number of people who may have different levels of interest in the report—they may want to gain a quick idea of the whole picture and then just refer to the detailed recommendations, or they may want a brief outline to give them a grasp of the topic before they give the report a detailed reading.

Writing a synopsis is no easy task, so if you *are* ever required to write one, give yourself sufficient time to do so—and remember it must be *brief* and confined to one page.

The Contents Page

A page listing the main sections and the numbers of the pages in the report on which they appear is only necessary if the report is a long one, where it is obviously an important guide to the reader. With a short report it is scarcely necessary, since it is unlikely to run to more than a few sides of paper. The contents page should be located at the front of the report before the synopsis.

USING THE WORD PROCESSOR FOR REPORTS

Two important aspects of producing an *effective* report is to create an overall impression that attracts the reader to open it and persuades him or her to read it and act on the contents. The development of word processing has done much to make reports more attractive. Visual impact can be created with a word processor or micro computer through:

- ▶ different typefaces
- ▶ changes of pitch, i.e. pica, elite, condensed
- ▶ emboldening features
- ▶ use of line spacing
- ▶ automatic tabs for progressive indentation
- ▶ use of graph symbols, asterisks, dots, dashes
- ▶ underlining

You can produce a template for the main sections of reports so that you always follow the correct sequence for presenting the information.

Word processing should also help you to improve the content of the report. The ability to edit on screen enables you to resist the temptation of clinging to the first draft. You can be more critical because the software will allow you to 'cut and paste', i.e. shift sections of text around until you have developed the most logical sequencing.

REPORT STYLE

Reports are formal documents, and the language should therefore be correct written English; it is not appropriate to include some of the more informal expressions we use in conversation. This is not to say it should be stilted or verbose—simply that it should be plain but accurate English.

It is also an impersonal document, so it should be presented in the third person; the only time that the use of 'I' is appropriate is in an eyewitness report—for example, if you have personally been present at the scene of an accident.

Lastly, it is important that reports should be written concisely—flowery expressions and long, complex sentences are to be avoided at all costs! These only serve to confuse the reader, and the use of complicated sentence structures and overlong words is often known as a 'high fog factor'—because it *does* befog the reader! You may remember that we discussed this before—it is just as important to aim for a low fog factor in reports as in letters.

CONCLUSION

Finally, remember that if a report is clearly set out and concisely written it is more immediately attractive to the eye, and more readable. After all your major objective is to ensure that your report is read! The principles we have discussed in this chapter should help you to achieve this goal.

ASSIGNMENTS

1 Information Report

You have now spent a year in your present employment. You have been asked to compile a brief information report for new recruits summarising the arrangements for initial training and coaching during the first year.

Your report should include information on induction arrangements, any training available externally (such as day-release or evening classes), any courses run by the bank itself. It should also include information on any arrangements which exist for coaching by experienced members of staff within the work place.

Task

Prepare the required report.

2 Investigation Report

The bank's management is concerned about the efficiency of the present communication methods used and about their costs. You have been asked to investigate the methods used by your branch and to study their suitability and cost-effectiveness. A report is to be submitted to your branch manager in which you:

(a) outline the methods of research and sources of information you have used;

(b) outline the current costs of communication methods you have researched;

(c) draw conclusions as to the cost-effectiveness and suitability of the methods;

(d) make recommendations as to how current costs could be reduced, or current methods be made more efficient.

You may also want to research new methods of communication which might make the communication system more efficient (you could refer back to the chapter and activities on Information Technology for this).

Task

Prepare the required report.

8 Effective Oral Presentation

Have you ever been asked to give a presentation—to a group of your colleagues, to a class at school/college, at a wedding or other similar occasion? You have to get up before a group of people, large or small, and speak for a few minutes to give them information, identify some problem, persuade them to take some course of action—and most of all, to get them to listen to you for those precious minutes.

SITUATIONS REQUIRING PRESENTATIONS

So far in your career at the bank, you may not have had to give a formal oral presentation. However, there are many work occasions when the need may arise. If you are attending college to gain qualifications, it is likely that part of your training will involve demonstrating the skill to get up in front of an audience and to speak for 5—30 minutes on a topic relevant to your work. As you progress within the bank, you may become involved in training or in the recruitment of new staff and these jobs will require you to talk to new employees/school-leavers about the work of your bank. Once you have subordinates, you will have to call meetings from time to time, some informal and some formal, in which you will have to pass on information to a group of people. You may be asked to investigate a particular aspect of the work of the bank and be asked to present an oral report on your findings to your superiors. You may even be asked, as your career progresses, to address students at colleges and universities about the financial services offered by the banks to various kinds of client. Almost certainly at some point in your career you will have to present certain services of the bank to a client or even to a group of clients.

Anxiety Associated with Oral Presentation

ACTIVITY 1
Pause for Thought

If you were asked to give an oral presentation, what worries would you have before the event?

It is a situation that most of us face with some trepidation—supposing the audience ignores us, or that we can't find the right words, or that they ask questions to which we have not researched the answers, or that we 'dry up' completely. For all but the most confident, the thought of having to give an oral presentation to a group of people works on the nerves and we are likely to experience a sleepless night, or even nightmares, worrying about whether everything will go right at the time.

To some extent being a little nervous can have a good effect if channelled positively to increase effort; it indicates that you are concerned and that you will have your mind finely tuned to what is required. Basically fear comes from the unknown. If you recognise this and prepare well for any oral presentation you will do a great deal to reduce uncontrolled nervousness which can, of course, have a negative result.

PREPARATION

It is true of many tasks that if a mistake is made in the early stages, everything else is likely to go wrong. You should remember this when planning your oral presentation. It is no good 'hoping' everything will go right when you get in the room—you must *plan* to ensure that it does go right. There are numerous areas for which you must plan—the subject-matter, the sequence of information, your notes, the time, the place, the audience, the audio-visual aids, etc. Let's start by considering why you are giving an oral presentation.

Objectives

The first question you must ask is:

Why am I giving a presentation? What purpose will it serve?

You need to know what you want your listeners to *do* as a result of the information you have given them. If you are giving an oral report to your superiors, for instance, you will want them to be able to take the appropriate action. Your purpose may be to provide information to a number of people so that they can understand the topic more fully. In more informal situations you may want to convey thanks to someone or, on social occasions, you may want to amuse.

Whatever the purpose of your presentation you need to be able to summarise your objective in one simple concise sentence. Once you have established what your ultimate objective is then as you progress in your planning you can use this objective as a test of relevance for the inclusion of information. Too often we merely identify as our objective in an oral presentation the ability to get through it without making too many errors!

Audience

The second question you must ask yourself is:

Who will be listening to me?

To be able to present information to an audience in the best possible way you need to find out something about them. You need to find out the approximate size of the audience, since it may affect the layout of your equipment and how loudly you will need to speak for everyone to hear. You need to know their existing knowledge about the subject—otherwise you may assume more knowledge than they possess and you will confuse them or you may underestimate their knowledge and run the risk of sounding patronising.

If you are going to give a presentation to a small group, take time to research their level of interest in the subject, their age, experience, prejudices. If they are work colleagues, superiors or subordinates you can probably find out this kind of information from someone who works closely with them. The more you know about your audience the better you can gear your vocabulary, style and tone to establishing a rapport with them. Sometimes it is difficult to know the required information about clients in advance and you will need to build up your knowledge of them when you meet them.

ACTIVITY 2

Pause for Thought

If you are following this course as part of a group, what do you already know about the other members of your group—attitudes, interests, behaviour, etc?

Use this information when you prepare for any presentation, oral or written, you make; it will help you to aim for your audience. Also reconsider these points when completing the assignment at the end of this chapter.

The problem with many presentations is that we 'skip through' these two stages of preparation too quickly. We have a vague idea of what we want to achieve and who our audience will be and then we rush on to thinking about content of the talk. Don't be tempted to hurry.

Producing a Schedule

The third question to ask is:

How long will it take me to prepare?

Depending on the nature of the presentation, there may be a number of activities to carry out before you actually deliver your talk. You will need to collect your information, organise the structure of your talk, write out your notes, check the room, check the equipment, produce visual aids, rehearse. If you have to do all this you would be wise to write out a *schedule* for yourself so that you can complete all your preparations in the time available. Work out how long each stage of preparation is likely to take you, e.g.:

Determining objectives and audience	1 hour
Researching audience	3 hours
Producing skeleton outline	1 hour
Collecting information	6 hours
Organising and writing up notes	3 hours
Producing audio-visual aids	1 hour
Checking room and equipment	½ hour
Dress rehearsal	1 hour

If this is your schedule you will need at least 16½ hours to fulfil it. Remember that the length of time you need to prepare will depend on the length and complexity of the material to be presented. It may be shorter or longer than the example given above. Depending on the number of days you have for preparation, you now need to work back from presentation day and time and allocate your time effectively. Obviously some factors may constrain your schedule. You may only be able to secure access to research information at certain times (e.g. if you are using a library); someone else may be preparing your visual aids for you and will need plenty of warning; you may have access to the room in which you are to give the talk at limited times—take all these factors into account in your schedule.

Collecting Information

The next question concerning preparation is:

What information do I need to collect?

Before you can research your talk you will need to determine a skeleton outline of the main points you want to make to your audience so that you have some framework for the collection of information. You are likely to revise this outline once you have accumulated all the facts and information you need.

While you are collecting your information you should check back to your identification of your objective and your type of audience so that you can begin distinguishing between relevant and irrelevant facts. You will be constantly collecting and sieving until you have facts which are directly relevant to the points you want to make. This selection process is extremely important. Always bear in mind that you are giving an oral presentation for the benefit of the audience not yourself. At all stages in the collection of your information consider what the audience might want to know, not just what you think they should be given. More detailed facts which you think might be of interest to only a few of your audience could be included by giving them a hand-out.

Preparing the Structure of the Talk

The information now needs to be presented in a logical way, so the next question is:

What is the most logical sequence for presenting this information to my audience?

ACTIVITY 3

Pause for Thought

What are the basic sections of any presentation?

There are a number of guidelines to help you with this. Every oral presentation needs:

(a) an introduction to the subject;
(b) the main body of the talk presenting the facts;
(c) a conclusion which repeats the main points and indicates any action to be taken.

Introduction This should tell your audience the purpose of your talk, the subject-matter, the structure you will be following, the time it will take and the methods of presentation you will use.

Main Body of the Talk Every talk requires quite original thought as to the exact sequence of the information you are presenting appropriate to the specific subject-matter. However, the starting point must always be the existing knowledge of the audience on which you can build.

If you are giving an oral report which is persuading your listeners to take a particular decision or course of action, it is useful to remember the five P's to provide the basic outline for your sequence. These are:

Purpose Identify the purpose of your talk

Position Identify the current situation

Problem Identify the problems which have arisen out of the current situation

Possibilities Outline the alternative courses of action open to the audience

Proposal State the course of action you are recommending

You will find this structure works effectively for any oral report you need to make and you should introduce this structure at the beginning of your presentation.

Conclusion This should remind your audience of the main points you made and, where relevant, the action you want them to take. In any case it should reiterate the priority points for their attention.

Example An example of an introduction which illustrates the kind of structure suitable for an oral report and which indicates its sequence is given below:

> Good morning, ladies and gentlemen. I would like to take up about 20 minutes of your time to make some proposals to you about introducing a new system for counter service at this branch. (Purpose) I will start by outlining our present position (Position) and by identifying the problems we have experienced in operating our present system. (Problems) I will then present a number of alternative methods of providing a counter service. (Possibilities) Finally, I will propose the system which I think will give the most efficient service to our customers. (Proposal) I shall be using a short video and a number of diagrams to illustrate my talk. If this is acceptable to you, I will start by outlining our present position . . .

Writing Notes

Up to this point you have probably made a lot of rough notes. Now you need to produce the notes from which you will give your talk. Some people are so concerned that they will forget what they want to say that they write out the whole of their oral presentation in longhand prose. This is not really a good idea because you will be tempted to 'read' your presentation rather than 'talk' to your audience.

ACTIVITY 4

Pause for Thought

Think back to the last time you listened to an oral presentation when the presenter read his/her talk and did not look at you.

What reactions did you have?

Somehow when a presentation is read to us we feel it somewhat insulting. We have bothered to come along to listen and the speaker cannot even acknowledge our presence by talking to us. It is also more difficult to believe in what is being said if the speaker does not have the conviction to look at us.

Notes for talks should conform to the principles we identified in Chapter 5 in the section on 'Making Notes'. You may also find the following guidelines helpful to writing notes for a talk:

(a) *Start with a rough draft*

Always produce a rough draft of your notes first. You are not likely to get the length, content or the sequence correct immediately and you will need to edit several times. Many people find it useful to mark paragraphs or sections of the first draft with the numbers 1, 2, or 3 to indicate the level of importance of the points being made. If length or content then has to be adjusted, you know that sections marked 3 should be deleted.

(b) *Opening*

The first few minutes of your talk are all-important since it is at this time that the audience expect you to establish a relationship with them. Unfortunately, it is also the stage at which 'nerves' hit you. For these reasons it is a good idea to write your introduction out in full and then memorise it.

(c) *Note cards*

Write your final set of notes on cards rather than paper—cards about 6in. × 4in. are ideal. Each card will have three or four points on it, written or printed in large letters so that you can read them quickly and easily. Thick felt pen and capital letters stand out at once. By having cards of this size you avoid trying to cram too much information on one page. It also has the advantage of being firmer so that your notes do not wave about (as you shake with nerves!). It is also a good idea to put a treasury tag through a hole in the corner of each card or some other securing device so that they are held together firmly in the right order—a great advantage if you drop your notes on the floor! (see page 156).

(d) *Schematic notes*

Ensure that you make maximum use of schematic layout for your notes with clear section headings, subheadings and numbered points (as described in Chapter 5).

(e) *Annotate your notes*

Oral presentations are one of the times when you need to annotate any notes you produce. Your annotations can be reminders about:

- the time you have allocated for each part of your talk

- when to use visual aid, i.e. turn on overhead projector (OHP), video
- when to use a special effect, e.g. make a joke, ask a question
- when to pass round a hand-out
- speed of delivery, e.g. SLOW DOWN! at a point where you want to achieve emphasis

(f) *Use signalling*

Since you want to be able to read information on your cards at a glance you must think carefully about how to make key points stand out on a page. Some helpful hints are:

- Space your information well.
- Use large printing that you can read easily.
- Highlight key words and phrases by use of colour printing, colour blocking or by underlining.

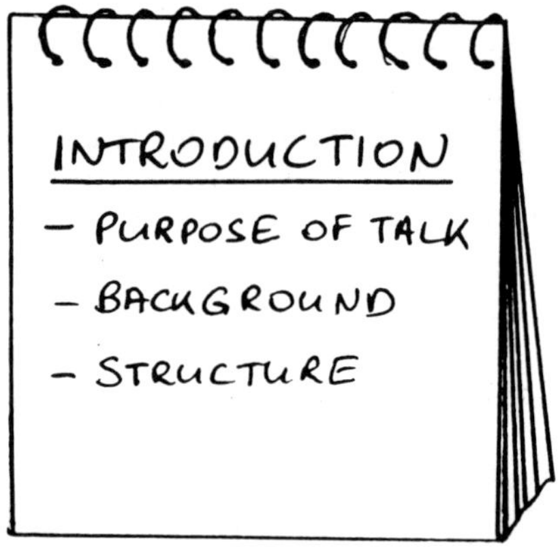

Note cards

Preparation of Visual Aids

It is often said that a picture is worth a thousand words. People can understand and remember information more easily if they can *see and hear.* This causes some presenters to overdo visual aids so that they virtually replace their words by overhead viewfoils, slides, charts and diagrams. You therefore need to consider each potential use of a visual aid very carefully and ask yourself:

*Do I really need a visual aid or can I manage **just as well** without it?*

Even if your first answer to this question is 'Yes', you need to go on to ask whether the visual aid you have in mind is really visual in terms of an illustration or are you merely transferring words from your mouth to a piece of paper or a viewfoil.

You should be using a visual aid because the subject-matter lends itself to visual impact, because it is impossible to convey an idea with words alone or because you can convey an idea more quickly and succinctly by a visual method. Below we cover some of the more common forms of visual aid you may be expected to employ, their uses and their problems.

Blackboard/Whiteboard This can be useful for building up a series of points in your talk or can be used for preprepared information. Do check up whether it is a black or whiteboard as you will need chalk for one and special pens for the other. In the latter case you will need a special board eraser—so do check up first.

Using a board successfully while talking needs practice. You need to be able to write clearly and quickly. If you have no time to practise in advance of your talk, avoid using this aid.

You have to turn round to write on a board and this means that:

(a) you have to turn your back partially on the audience, which will affect your audibility if you are still talking; and

(b) you can obscure information you may have already put on the board.

Some tips for using boards to present information and ideas are:

- Practise.
- Go to your presentation equipped with chalk or pens, eraser, plus pointer.
- Plan your use of the board so that during your talk you do not have to write for more than a few seconds at a time.
- If you already have information on the board and you are talking about it, remember to stand at the side of the board, facing the audience and then point to the relevant words, using a pointer.

Overhead Projector (OHP) This has become a popular visual aid in offices, boardrooms, training suites and classrooms. It involves preparing information on a transparent viewfoil. When the viewfoil is placed on the overhead projector and the projector is switched on the image is projected and magnified on to a screen. This aid has some advantages over boards since viewfoils can be prepared in advance, the projector can be used facing the audience and the information is magnified on to a screen so that it can be easily seen from all points of a room. The OHP is also very useful for displaying cartoons, charts, diagrams and pictures.

However, there are also inherent difficulties in using the OHP. Many presenters try to crowd too much information on one viewfoil by writing very small so that the audience has difficulty in reading and absorbing all the information. You will also find that putting a viewfoil on the projector, positioning it correctly, turning the projector on, all takes time and concentration and this may break the flow of what you are saying.

Since the image on the screen (which will be behind and to the side of the presenter) will be larger than on the viewfoil itself, there is a temptation for the presenter to turn round and talk to the points which appear on the screen. You will also find that bad presenters position themselves between the OHP and the screen so that the information is obscured.

Some tips on using the OHP are:

- Try out your finished viewfoils on the OHP before your presentation so that you know the image is right in size and impact.
- Practise with the OHP so that you are familiar with how it works and you are not fumbling around on the day.
- Check the layout of the room and position the OHP and screen in such a position that when you are standing beside it you are not obscuring anyone's view.
- Place your viewfoils in the order that you will use them alongside where you are standing. Immediately you have finished with a viewfoil, place it on the other side of the OHP so that they cannot get mixed up.
- Make sure you position yourself by the side of the OHP and that you do not move between the OHP and the screen.
- Give the audience sufficient time to absorb the information on the viewfoil but when you have finished take it off the OHP immediately and then turn the projector off until you show the next one. A finished viewfoil or a blank lighted screen are both distractions to an audience, as is the noise the OHP fan makes.

Flip-chart A flip-chart consists of a pad of large-sized paper attached to a firm backing board. Once one sheet of paper has been written on, it is 'flipped over' revealing the next sheet of paper. It is possible to preprepare flip-chart information but generally it is used as a method of building up information as you go along. Many people avoid using this aid as it means writing in front of an audience. You may also find that your writing is too small for the audience to see the detail.

It is an excellent medium for displaying key words or phrases that you want the audience to remember while you talk about one aspect of the topic or for rough sketches. Some tips on using flip-charts are:

- ▶ Make sure the flip-chart is at a suitable height for writing comfortably.
- ▶ If you prepare your flip-chart information in advance, try to leave a blank sheet in between sheets of information so that you do not display new information too early by mistake.
- ▶ Use large printing and bold coloured pens so that the information shows up clearly.

As your career progresses you may need to use more sophisticated equipment, such as slide projector, video recorder or film projector. Always contact such expert staff as are available in your organisation who can advise you on the use of the equipment—and *practise first*.

ACTIVITY 5

Exercise

What audio-visual methods would you use for the following:

(a) to show the number of new account holders for your branch over the past six months;
(b) to build up a list of key points (by asking the audience) on handling awkward customers;
(c) to show the office layout of your branch;
(d) to show, in a dramatic way, how to give a good oral presentation.

You do not have to confine your answers to methods identified in the text. Some ideas are given in the suggested answer at the end of the chapter.

Language

Spoken English One aspect you need to consider very carefully before you deliver your presentation is the language you will use. Although many talks may be a formal occasion you need to use different sentence construction and vocabulary from written reports or letters.

Spoken English is not full of multi-syllable words, turgid phrases and complicated sentences. It is simple, concise and direct. We talk in short, simple sentences without long involved dependent clauses. We have licence to break some of the rules considered important in written English, e.g. finishing a sentence with a preposition. We use vernacular phrases, i.e. slang, and we use the first and second person 'I' and 'you' instead of the more impersonal third person 'he', 'she' or 'it'.

As you produce your *written draft* you need to make sure you are preparing that draft using *spoken English*. If you don't you will find that your presentation sounds stilted and over-formal. Include some of your best phrases in your notes.

ACTIVITY 6

Exercise

The following is an extract from the first three sections of a written Health and Safety at Work report carried out within your bank which you (as the Safety Representative) are asked to present orally at a meeting briefly and concisely.

1 *Introduction*

The Health and Safety Officer visited the premises of the National Eastern Bank PLC at Ockingham on 9 December 19—— to ascertain whether acceptable standards were being upheld. His report was submitted to the manager of the branch on 20 December 19—— for his immediate attention.

2 *Methods*

The Health and Safety Officer visited the above premises for one day. He employed the following methods:

2.1 He observed the present conditions concerning temperature, ventilation, special hazards, working space, hygiene facilities.

2.2 He interviewed a cross-section of each department to gain their views/knowledge of safety procedures and health standards.

2.3 He secured copies of safety policy documents and notices in use at present.

3 *Analysis of present situation and problems arising*

3.1 *Conditions of work*—generally the heating and lighting levels were found to be acceptable according to the provisions of the Act but the following special hazards were identified:

3.1.1 trailing leads on electronic equipment;
3.1.2 badly placed plug points;

3.1.3 waste-paper baskets used as ash trays by staff;
3.1.4 no directions on filing cabinets concerning the correct sequence for opening drawers to avoid tipping;
3.1.5 loose mats on polished floors.

3.2 . . .

Convert this extract to concise spoken English aimed at an audience of the bank manager, his assistant and chief cashier.

A suggested answer is given at the end of the chapter.

Words for Signposting One feature of written communication is that the reader can take his/her time to make sense of what is written. He/she can use aids, such as subheadings, to know when to move from one aspect of the topic to another. In preparing an oral presentation, you must think how you can fulfil this same function using spoken English. You need to provide 'verbal signposts' to help your audience make the switch from one train of thought to another. For example:

> I hope I *have outlined* the main problems associated with the present system. I would now like to *move on to consider* some of the alternative systems we might use.

Rehearse

Your next stage is to rehearse the talk you have prepared. First become familiar with the content and the words you want to use; then consider your posture, gestures, tone and pace. Practise in front of a mirror so that you can see what you look like; practise with a cassette recorder so that you play your talk back and listen critically to the pace and tone. If you can secure the cooperation of a friend, ask them to listen to you and to comment on what you say, how you say it, how you look.

Venue

Lastly, make sure the room in which you will give your talk is prepared properly for your purpose. *Don't rely* on someone else having set up the furniture and equipment as you want them—check it yourself. You should already have decided before this point on the optimum layout and tried to secure this (although admittedly sometimes you may not be able to choose the ideal layout). If you can, try to avoid having the audience at a great distance from you—it only emphasises the formality of the occasion and you will have to speak louder! If it is important that you maintain eye contact with each member of your audience (i.e. if you are addressing a small group, arrange the chairs in such a manner that maintaining this contact is easy for you). Make sure there is somewhere you can place your notes—and still be able to read them. If you have to use a microphone, or in fact any equipment, check that it is working properly.

DELIVERY

A successful presentation consists of addressing a mass of people using the voice, gesture, and posture techniques that you use, unconsciously, when talking to a group of friends. Unfortunately, the self-consciousness which strikes us in front of an audience often creates a fixed or glazed expression, paralysis of the vocal chords and gestures/posture which makes us look like a wooden puppet! You will find that successful presenters have the range of facial expressions and gestures we use in familiar situations and they have good variety in the pace and tone of their voices.

In the next few sections of this chapter we have included some techniques to help you towards good delivery.

ACTIVITY 7

Exercise

Make a list of all the effective and ineffective techniques of giving an oral presentation.

You can use, for observation, the presentations of past teachers/lecturers, training personnel within the bank, television presenters, speakers at wedding receptions or formal dinners, politicians.

You should consider the effects of their voices, mannerisms, posture, gestures and facial expressions.

Voice

You need to aim first for *audibility*, which means clear diction and a slightly slower pace than normal conversation. Good legible notes help here since you can refer to them briefly, keeping *your head up*, which means that your voice is projected forward to the audience.

You also need to aim for *variety of tone*. A monotone will send any audience to sleep—as you may have experienced yourself. Practise on tape is invaluable here even if you are horrified the first time you hear yourself—a common reaction! In your anxiety to finish your talk as quickly as possible you may fall into the trap of gabbling, which is both irritating and confusing for an audience. Alternatively, lack of confidence may cause you to mumble or to lose the ends of words or sentences by dropping your voice.

Remember the phrase 'Don't be a mumbler or a gabbler' and avoid these faults by aiming for:

- clear pronunciation of each word
- lifting your voice at the ends of sentences
- variety in tone and pace

Eye Contact

To maintain eye contact is particularly important since it establishes a rapport with the audience and allows you to interact with them. It is important because it gives recognition to the audience—they can be forgiven for thinking you are ignoring them if you stare out of the window, at the ceiling or at the floor. This is insulting and likely to be resented. Eye contact is also important because it allows you to gauge their response to what you are saying; if their eyes are glazed, for example, it is likely that they are bored or confused. Only by observing the audience's reaction can you adjust your approach.

Being sensitive to the audience is a necessary prerequisite to effective presentation, as any actor will tell you, so:

- Make sure you look at your audience.

Expression

People respond to your expression instantly. If you appear enthusiastic, interested and motivated and your expression is alert and responsive, they are much more likely to share that interest and enthusiasm. The English tend to have rather immobile facial expressions which unfortunately convey lack of interest. Watch the French or Italians and, even if you don't know their language, you usually know what they are trying to convey. Most successful presenters use their facial expressions and features with mobility to convey amusement, humour, fascination, horror, anger, anxiety.

Practising in front of a mirror may give you some idea of how you appear to others but if you get the opportunity to do a practice presentation which is video-recorded, the playback is the biggest eye-opener of all. A common reaction is to see yourself as stiff and wooden and once this is recognised you can begin to adjust your behaviour. You might like to reread the section on body language in Chapter 1 to remind yourself of the reactions people may have to expressions and voice.

Remember to use every opportunity to watch your own facial expressions so that you can practise and can:

▶ Use a range of facial expressions to reinforce your words.

Gesture

Again, the English are more controlled about their gestures than most and no one would wish to recommend the style adopted by some dictators who have used gesture to intimidate an audience or forcibly put across a point. There are some people, too, who suffer from a ludicrous over-use of gesture which merely looks ridiculous. On the other hand, the use of gestures which are economic and descriptive can aid the understanding and interest of the audience.

They can be used to emphasise, explain and demonstrate, sometimes more effectively than words alone. In some situations this becomes quite evident. For instance, try directing or instructing someone without using gestures—you will find it difficult for you to do and often difficult for him/her to understand. Remember that gestures should accompany words and not act as their substitute. A vague wave of the hand and a feeble phrase such as 'You know what I mean' usually ensures that your audience does not understand!

▶ Use economic and descriptive gestures to emphasise, explain and demonstrate, but ensure they *accompany* words.

Mannerisms

All of us have seen people give a public presentation where a repeated mannerism has proved distracting and irritating. Common ones include:

▶ jingling money or keys

▶ fidgeting with jewellery or pens

▶ pacing up and down the floor

- repeated use of 'Um', 'Ah', 'You know' or 'Well'

- finger drumming or clicking

to name but a few. Perhaps you can think of others. Feedback from other people or a video-recording can help you to identify any persistent mannerisms.

Once you are aware of these you are in a better position to reduce or eliminate them.

Stance and Posture

Inexperienced speakers often find it difficult to adopt an upright and confident posture. They tend to slouch, lean on the desk or wall, stoop, stand on one foot or fidget nervously. Some people are afraid that the audience can see them shaking! Whether you sit or stand for your presentation is sometimes dictated by the formality of the occasion or the position of the audience. However, if you have a choice and you feel more confident in a sitting position it may be better to adopt this. Nevertheless, you should always practise a standing delivery as sometimes it will be the only one which is appropriate.

An upright, calm and controlled posture communicates confidence to the audience and shows respect for them. A slouching or over-casual stance has the opposite effect. It is also easier to breathe slowly and evenly if you are standing or sitting upright.

- Adopt an upright and confident posture.

Appearance

Of course, general appearance, dress, tidiness is important, too. You should wear neat yet comfortable clothes. An oral presentation is not the time to break in a new pair of shoes or wear some outfit with a very tight waistband! However, if you know you look good it will help to improve your image and your confidence.

Involvement of Audience

Sometimes you may be addressing specific people on specific issues or you may wish to involve people in your audience by asking questions—or indeed you may have to answer questions from the audience. Remember that this involves a constant response to their needs and interests. A dialogue with the audience can be valuable in promoting understanding, interest and action so long as you treat them with tact and diplomacy.

Personal Qualities

There are a number of qualities which you will need to convey to the audience if your talk is to be successful. These are:

(a) *Your own interest and expertise in the subject*—enthusiasm is infectious and a well-rehearsed presentation always commands respect.

(b) *Honesty and sincerity*—the audience need to believe and trust what you say. If you are asked a question to which you do not know the answer, it is better to admit that you don't know but will find out and inform them than to try to bluff your way through an inaccurate or vague answer. Once again an audience will respect honesty and will respond to it.

(c) *Humour*—an audience likes to enjoy a presentation and, if the subject allows, to be amused and entertained. However, humour needs to be handled very sensitively in response to an audience's reactions if it is to be effective. If they share your humour they will enjoy and remember what you had to say but if they do not share your humour they will withdraw mentally and begin to doubt the sincerity of your words.

CONCLUSION: CHECK-LISTS

Since we have given you a considerable amount of detail about the preparation and delivery of oral presentations, it might be useful to summarise the main points by giving you two check-lists.

Preparation

(1) Determine your objectives.

(2) Identify and research your audience.

(3) Produce a preparation schedule to make sure you cover every aspect and that you are ready in time.

(4) Collect information—sieve and retain relevant information only.

(5) Determine the most logical structure using the five P's.

(6) Produce clear, concise schematic notes.

(7) Decide on the most relevant visual techniques and prepare visual aids.

(8) Check language to ensure talk is in spoken English and that you are providing verbal signposts.

(9) Rehearse.

(10) Check venue.

Delivery

(1) Pronounce words clearly.

(2) Speak a little more slowly than normal.

(3) Try to vary pace and tone.

(4) Maintain eye contact and *talk to* your audience.

(5) Try to use a variety of facial expressions to reinforce words.

(6) Use gestures which are economic and descriptive to emphasise, explain and demonstrate.

(7) Maintain a good upright posture.

(8) Avoid annoying mannerisms.

(9) Dress—look good but be comfortable.

(10) Practice makes perfect.

SUGGESTED ANSWERS TO ACTIVITIES

Activity 5

(a) In this situation you could use a bar chart on an OHP, black/whiteboard or on a flip-chart.

(b) You could build up your key points during the presentation on a black/whiteboard or on a flip-chart as the audience volunteers specific points.

(c) There are a number of ways you could do this by preparing in advance: a scale model, slides, a short video (ambitious methods) or diagram on an OHP viewfoil, flip-chart or board (simpler methods).

(d) You could incorporate a suitable video into your presentation, or act out the right and wrong techniques. You could incorporate voices recorded on a cassette recorder.

Activity 6

Spoken English might be as follows:

> When the Health and Safety Officer visited our branch on the 9th of December he was reasonably satisfied with our standards.

He spent a day with us looking at our heating, ventilation, etc., and talking to staff in each department about their views on our health and safety standards. He took away with him copies of our policy documents and safety notices.

We received his written report on the 20th. Unfortunately, he listed a number of hazards. Our computers have leads trailing across the floor because plug sockets are badly placed. Some of our staff tend to use wastepaper baskets as ash trays, creating a fire hazard! We have several loose mats on our polished floors which could cause accidents. We do not have any warning notices on our filing cabinets about the dangers of opening more than one drawer at once. On the good side, he did find our heating and lighting satisfactory!

ASSIGNMENT

Find the notes you made for Activity 4 of Chapter 5 on note-making. Reduce and edit these on to cards and annotate according to the visual aids and hand-outs which you would wish to use in your five-minute presentation.

Prepare appropriate visual aids and/or hand-outs. You are being required to give your presentation at a date, time and place designated by your tutor. You should assume that your audience will be the school 5th-formers described in the activity. Go through the preparation check-list to ensure that you have carried out each stage satisfactorily.

Deliver your talk as required using your cards and visual aids. Discuss your performance with the rest of your class and your tutor.

In terms of self-assessment and improvement you should take into account the comments of your tutor/audience and/or a video or cassette recording of your performance.

9 Meetings

INTRODUCTION

What kind of activity do you associate with the word 'meeting'? At the simplest level, it describes an encounter, by chance or arrangement, between one or more people—for example, with a group of friends in the street. At a more complex level, it is a formal gathering of specific people to decide on particular matters by means of set procedures—for example, the board meeting of a company. Research has shown that people who rise to managerial positions in business organisations spend about 50 per cent of their work time in meetings of one sort or another and this makes the conduct of meetings a very expensive activity in terms of man-hours involved.

You may be one of those people who feel that all the time spent in meetings tends to be unproductive and that many of them are a waste of time. This indicates that some meetings may not really be necessary—the decision could be made more effectively by one person—or that the meeting is run inefficiently so that the participants get bored, frustrated or irritated.

ACTIVITY 1

Pause for Thought

Think of any meetings you may have attended—at school, social club, work, etc. If you have experienced any of the negative reactions mentioned above, try to identify and list some of the faults that contributed to this reaction.

Then read on and compare your list with ours.

You may have listed any of the following:

- You were not given sufficient information in advance to participate in the meeting properly.
- You were given too much information and you could not make sense of it all.
- A decision already seemed to have been made and you wondered why you had been asked to attend.
- The person chairing/leading the meeting failed to control the meeting.
- Individual members kept going off the point.

- The discussion kept on going round in circles.
- No one appeared to be recording any of the decisions made.
- There were some people who dominated the discussion while other people could not/would not say anything.
- There was obvious conflict between two individuals which got out of hand.

This is not an exhaustive list but does give some indication of common faults of meetings. If such faults are so common, it raises the question of whether we need to have meetings at all.

PURPOSE OF MEETINGS

We have described what can occur if meetings are not organised or conducted properly but if meetings are conducted well they can make a significant contribution to the communication system of the organisation. Business is not just concerned with making decisions but also with informing people of decisions, securing their acceptance and getting people to act on those decisions.

ACTIVITY 2

Pause for Thought

If meetings are well organised and conducted, what functions can they perform effectively? You might like to reflect here and note your own answers before continuing to read.

Meetings can fulfil one or more of the functions listed below; you may have thought of several of these:

- To arrive at a decision which is *agreed* by all those who are responsible for putting it into effect.
- To consult others and to find out opinions and attitudes before an individual makes a decision.
- To pool ideas when it is necessary to create new ideas or to solve a problem (on the basis that two or more heads are better than one!).
- To plan work load, allocate tasks according to expertise and interest or to discuss work progress.
- To prepare or train employees for new work or procedures.
- To inform a number of people at the same time.

- To negotiate an agreement which represents the interests of two or more groups of people.
- To carry out an investigation.
- Deliberately to spread the responsibility for a decision.

A meeting will not fulfil *all* these purposes. Each type of meeting should have its own specific purposes. It is therefore important that you can recognise the different types of meeting in order to identify the purposes they may serve.

TYPES OF MEETING

In simple terms, we can categorise meetings as formal or informal. In order to determine which category is suitable for a particular meeting, you can use the following table to help you make your choice:

Formal	*Informal*
It has some form of written constitution which determines its rules and procedures.	There is no formal constitution; members decide how they will conduct it.
The meeting is formally documented: ▶ notice of meeting ▶ agenda ▶ motions ▶ minutes.	There are no formal documents: ▶ meeting called by telephone, memo or personal contact ▶ someone may be nominated to take notes.
Follows formal rules and procedures for the conduct of the meeting which are laid down in the constitution.	There are no formal rules; the person calling the meeting must decide how to run it.
There is special terminology used.	No special terminology.
The meeting has special officers: ▶ chairperson ▶ secretary ▶ treasurer.	There are no special officers; the person calling the meeting is likely to act as leader.
There is a definite method of making decisions—voting.	Decisions arise out of common agreement or result in manager making an individual decision after consulting others in the meeting.

Although the table is a useful guide to identification, you will soon appreciate that it is very difficult to fit a particular meeting into one of the two categories. It may have elements of both. It may be an informal meeting that is becoming recognised within the organisation and therefore begins to adopt *some* of the features of a formal meeting. It is therefore probably more useful to think of meetings in terms of *degree* of formality. This is illustrated in the following diagram which shows some of the typical meetings which may take place in your own bank.

Most formal ◄	*Some formality* ◄	*Least formal*
Board meeting	Branch	Information giving
Shareholders	Departmental	Briefing
Employer/trade union or staff association	Section	Problem solving
	Project team	

Types of meeting

In order to link types of meeting with their purposes, you should attempt the following activity.

ACTIVITY 3

Exercise

Look back to the list of purposes of meetings shown on page 169. For each of the types of meeting listed below, write down the main purpose(s) of the meeting:

(a) briefing meeting by superior;
(b) employer/trade union or staff association meeting;
(c) problem-solving meeting;
(d) directors' meeting;
(e) social committee meeting.

Then compare your answers with the ones that appear at the end of the chapter.

You are likely to be required to participate in a number of different types of meeting in your early career, and identifying the type of meeting helps you to decide what is required of you. You will need to know a little about their conduct and procedures. In the next few sections we will deal with the organisation and conduct of both formal and informal meetings.

ORGANISATION AND CONDUCT OF MEETINGS

Formal Meetings

In the early stages of your career you may not be required to participate in the most formal meetings in your organisation. However, the Chartered Institute of Bankers recognises that as you progress you do need to know how to conduct yourself within this environment. You therefore need to become familiar with the documents, terminology and procedures used. Even though you may not be allowed to attend the formal meetings conducted within your own work place, there are still plenty of opportunities to see the formalities in practice. You can go along to your local authority's council meetings which are open to the public. If you belong to a social club, ask to look at its constitution. Formal company meetings will be subject to legal requirements under the Companies Act 1985 and to a number of EC directives.

Documentation for Formal Meetings The basic documents of the formal meeting are:

(a) the notice of meeting;
(b) the agenda;
(c) the chairperson's agenda;
(d) the minutes of the meeting.

Let us now look at what each should contain and the regulations to which they should conform.

(a) *Notice of Meeting*

Before a formal meeting can be held, a notice of meeting must be given/sent to those who are entitled to attend. This notice can only be sent by the person authorised to call the meeting (in the constitution). This is usually the chairperson, although the notice is often signed by the secretary—see the example of a notice of meeting shown on page 174.

As you can see, the notice must show the title of the meeting, the date, time and place. It will specify whether an agenda of the meeting is attached. It will be signed with an indication of that person's official position within the group.

A notice of meeting is usually sent well ahead of the meeting's date (usually 21 days) so that members can keep the date and time free and so that they can prepare themselves for the meeting. Often the notice required for the meeting is laid down in the constitution.

Example of notice of meeting and agenda

NATIONAL EASTERN BANK PLC

NOTICE OF MEETING: SOUTHERN REGION SOCIAL AND SPORTS ASSOCIATION

A meeting of the above association will be held on Tuesday 7 May 19.. at 7.30 p.m. in the Conference Room of the Finchester Leisure Centre. Members representing all local branches within the region are invited to attend. The agenda is enclosed.

Signed:

Secretary

Enc. Agenda

NATIONAL EASTERN BANK PLC

Meeting of the Southern Region Social and Sports Association to be held Tuesday 7 May 19.. at 7.30 p.m.
Venue: Conference Room, Finchester Leisure Centre

AGENDA

1. Apologies for absence
2. Minutes of last meeting
3. Matters arising
4. Correspondence: Sports fixtures for June-September
5. Treasurer's Report
6. Social Subcommittee's Report: Arrangements for the July Ball
7. Discussion on the motion: 'That a reduced membership fee should be charged to members under 18'.
   Proposed: Miss B.L. Young (Ockingham Branch)
   Seconded: Mr L.R. Yates (Newtown Branch)
8. Any Other Business
9. Date of next meeting

A notice of meetings may now be sent by E-mail. Meetings schedules are often part of a management information system software operating on LANs and WANs. This software provides a pre-designed format for calling a meeting. The relevant information can be keyed in and then transmitted simultaneously to all participants, both internal and (if necessary) external.

It is also possible to have fast checking of availability for meetings through E-mail so that a suitable date and time can be fixed. Software enables the person calling the meeting to access each participant's electronic diary for the date and time and then block in the meeting time so that double-bookings cannot occur.

(b) *Agenda*

Since members need to prepare for a meeting if it is to be effective, it is important that they have some idea of the matters to be discussed and the order in which various items will be handled. The agenda serves this purpose. It is usually prepared by the secretary in consultation with the chairperson. In many cases the agenda will be distributed at the same time as the notice of meeting. If the agenda is to be distributed after the notice of meeting, the initial notice may ask members to submit items for discussion so that they can be included on the agenda. Fast distribution of agendas can be achieved in an organisation using E-mail.

The items which may typically appear on an agenda which enable the members to see the outline of the meeting are:

- Apologies for absence
- Minutes of last meeting to be read and approved
- Matters arising from minutes
- Reading of correspondence received which relates to meeting
- Any business postponed from the last meeting
- Presentation of reports/accounts before the meeting for adoption or approval

- Special business to be discussed—items are likely to be listed separately, or
- Consideration/discussion of motions (if these have been submitted in advance)
- Any other business
- Date of next meeting

An example of an agenda was shown on page 174 with the notice of meeting.

(c) *Chairperson's Agenda*

Since it is the chairperson's role to lead and control the meeting (see page 178) it is usual to have a special version of the agenda which helps the chairperson to conduct the meeting quickly and efficiently. This agenda should be agreed between the secretary and the chairperson a few days before the meeting takes place.

This agenda shows additional information which will be of value to the chairperson during the meeting. It will include some timings for the various sections to be covered, together with some reminder notes. There is usually a space left on the right-hand side of the page against each item on the agenda so that the chairperson can make brief notes. If there are any documents, papers to be discussed during the meeting, these should be attached to the chairperson's agenda. An example of a chairperson's agenda is shown on page 177.

(d) *Minutes*

All the above documents are necessary *before* the meeting takes place. The minutes, which record what happened at the meeting and what decisions were made, are produced very shortly after the meeting and are then distributed to the members. Minutes usually appear in the same order as the agenda with clear, numbered subheadings. They give the basic facts and the resolutions reached. Some more detailed hints on minute writing are given later in this chapter (see pages 182–9).

The table on page 178 shows the sequence for preparing and distributing meetings documents.

Example of chairperson's agenda

NATIONAL EASTERN BANK PLC

Meeting of the Southern Region Social and Sports Association to be held on Tuesday 7 May 19-- at 7.30 p.m.
Venue: Conference Room, Finchester Leisure Centre.

CHAIRPERSON'S AGENDA

Approx. time	Agenda Item	Notes in Preparation	Notes from the Meeting
7.30	1. Apologies for absence	Mrs M. Keith (Burbridge) M.P. Evans (Lowton): on holiday	
7.31	2. Minutes	Circulate, take as read.	
7.33	3. Matters arising	Ask if anyone wishes to make a point.	
7.40	4. Correspondence	Secretary circulated fixtures. NB post to Burbridge and Lowton branches.	
7.45	5. Treasurer's Report	Circulated, take a resolution of acceptance.	
7.50	6. Social Sub-committee's Report: Arrangements for July Ball	Ask Chairman of Sub-committee for oral report. Note arrangements.	
8.10	7. Motion: 'that a reduced membership fee should be charged to members under 18'. Proposed: Miss B.L. Young (Ockingham) Seconded: L.R. Yates (Newtown)	Discuss amount of reduction; take addendum or amendment; take vote.	
8.30	8. Any Other Business	None known at present. Ask members for any they wish to raise.	
8.40	9. Date of next meeting	Suggest 8 June 19.. Venue: Porthampton Sports Centre.	

Preparation for a formal meeting

Before

28—21 days	Secretary despatches notice of meeting to members. Secretary circulates minutes of last meeting.
21—14 days	Items to be included on the agenda are forwarded to the secretary.
14—7 days	Chairperson and secretary agree agenda. Secretary despatches agenda to members. Secretary prepares chairperson's agenda.
7—0 days	Secretary finalises preparations for meeting—room, documents, correspondence, etc. Secretary finalises up-to-date chairperson's agenda.

After

0—7 days	Chairperson and secretary check records of meeting. Secretary produces draft minutes.

Official Roles within Formal Meetings

Chairperson
In all formal meetings there is someone appointed by a superior body or elected by the members who controls the conduct of the meeting. This is the chairperson. The way the chairperson assumes the role will be defined in a document known as the *constitution* (although you may come across the term *articles* or *standing orders*).

ACTIVITY 4
Pause for Thought

You have probably observed people who have taken the chair at a formal meeting. You may even have been elected to a chairperson's role yourself within a social or sports committee.

What do you see as being the main tasks and responsibilities that a chairperson should undertake?

You may have thought of a number of the following powers and duties in the activity above. The powers and duties of a chairperson are likely to include:

- *Preparing for the meeting* This includes authorising the agenda for distribution to members and checking the chairperson's agenda and practical arrangements for the meeting.

- *Familiarising him/herself with the procedures* laid down in the constitution document.

- *Opening the meeting* and ensuring that a quorum is present (a quorum means the minimum number of people that the constitution document states must be present).

- The members should be welcomed and the purpose of the meeting should be stated.

- The chairperson should make the apologies of members who cannot attend the meeting and should secure the approval of the minutes of the last meeting and sign these as having been approved.

- *Conducting the meeting* The chairperson should follow the rest of the agenda (see page 177) within the time allocations as far as possible. He/she should also:

  —keep the discussion relevant
  —summarise discussions to prevent repetition
  —keep discussion orderly
  —help to word motions and amendments (see page 181–82)
  —make decisions on procedural matters
  —take votes and declare results
  —adjourn meeting (when necessary), i.e. give a short break
  —ensure agreement has been reached

- *Closing the meeting* and giving a date for the next meeting.

NB A vice-chairperson may be appointed/elected but takes no particular official role unless the chairperson is absent.

You may have realised that the role of chairperson requires considerable abilities to lead and control a meeting. These aspects are dealt with later in the section on pages 190–196.

Secretary

This is a very important role since the secretary carries out all the administrative and communication functions associated with the meeting by handling documents and records and making the practical arrangements for holding the meeting. You should never confuse the role of committee secretary with that of a private secretary. The secretary of, say, a committee carries out the following duties:

- Preparing the notice of meeting and agenda, ensuring that they are circulated to the members; preparing the chairperson's agenda in consultation with the chairperson.
- Prompting of the chairperson on whether the meeting is being conducted according to the constitution and meetings procedure.
- Ensuring that a record is made of the meeting and that this becomes the basis of formal minutes to be distributed to all members, and entering the minutes in the minute book.
- Carrying out the communication/administrative work necessitated by the meeting.

As the secretary is an observer and recorder of the meeting, he/she does not take an active part in the discussions of the meeting itself but the precise role will be defined by the constitution.

The qualities and skills demanded in a secretary are administrative and organisational. He/she will also need to have acute listening skills and the ability to summarise information effectively. These skills have been discussed earlier and you will find them useful if you have to be a meetings secretary.

Other official roles

The need for other officers may vary according to the type of meeting required. It is likely that they will be stated in the constitution. The one that you are most likely to encounter is that of *treasurer* who, as the name implies, controls the accounts and submits financial reports.

Members

The responsibilities and duties of ordinary members are unfortunately often neglected. Too many turn up to the meeting without having prepared themselves and participate without much forethought. It is perhaps because of this that it has been said that 'the camel is a horse designed by a committee', and the phrase 'having given this matter a great deal of thought' has been unkindly interpreted as meaning 'off the top of my head'.

Conscientious members, however, are very important in the communication process for they will observe their responsibilities which are crucial to good decision-making and information. These are listed below:

- *Preparing for the meeting* The agenda needs to be studied and any facts or arguments concerning each item collected in advance. This is particularly important if you are representing other people since you will have to consult them for views before attending the meeting. Where figures, data or other detailed information is needed by other members, they should be brought to the meeting in such a form that enables them to be displayed or handed round.

▶ *Participating in the meeting* It has often been said that members should 'stand up, speak up and shut up'. Certainly it is helpful to the official running of the meeting if you can state concisely what you wish to say and you can also listen and respond intelligently to what others have said. You should avoid:

—hogging the discussion
—shouting others down
—repeating yourself
—interrupting other members

It is worth noting that in formal meeting procedure, each member should 'address the chair' rather than talking directly across the table. If you are unsure of a point of procedure you should consult the chairperson and nobody else. Each member should take his/her own notes of the meeting.

▶ *After the meeting* Members should ensure any action delegated to them is carried out. If you are representing other people, you should report back on what has occurred at the meeting and why.

There are sometimes additional special members in a meeting. These are defined in the glossary at the end of this chapter as *ex officio* members and *co-opted* members.

Procedure and Terminology We have already mentioned in this chapter one or two terms connected with the procedure of meetings (for example, quorum on page 179). There are unfortunately a large number of terms which describe the procedures of formal meetings. Because there are so many of these we have defined them briefly in a glossary (pages 200–204). If you are involved in attending a formal meeting you can use this glossary as a reference source. It is advisable, however, to learn as many of these as possible since knowledge in this area is often tested.

One procedure to which it is worth giving further attention is that which leads from the formulation of a motion to voting on a resolution. This can be described as follows:

(a) *Motion* A meeting is usually held to discuss possible actions and to decide how they should be carried out. Each topic to be considered is called a motion or proposal. It is usually phrased in such terms as, 'It is proposed that a sports centre should be established.' It is always proposed by a member but must also be seconded (or supported) by another member before it can be discussed or put to the vote.

(b) *Amendments* Sometimes another member will wish to amend (or change) the original proposal or motion in some way. For example, he/she may wish to propose that a sports club be established for junior employees only. In this case the amendment must have a proposer and a seconder and must be voted on first. If the amendment is passed the motion becomes known as a *substantive motion*.

(c) *Voting* Voting is usually carried out by a show of hands. A member may vote 'for' or 'against' a motion or may 'abstain' (the latter means that he/she does not vote at all). In some cases where the vote is exactly even, the chairperson may be empowered to use a *casting vote* at his/her discretion. Terms connected with various kinds of votes are given in the glossary. Very occasionally a secret vote is taken by ballot or poll, where there may be vested interests or other pressures.

(d) *Resolution* This is the decision which is finally taken and will be recorded in the minutes, often together with the vote.

The procedure shown above is highlighted in the flow chart on page 183.

Writing Minutes As a meeting is in progress, the secretary will need to ensure that a record of the proceedings is taken down. These will be written up after the meeting and will form the minutes. In some very formal meetings this record will be entered in a *minutes book*.

Minutes follow the same order as the agenda and they must be an accurate record of what was said and agreed. They need to be written down in concise note form as they are *not* a blow-by-blow account. Occasionally *verbatim minutes* may be required; these are an exact record of everything that was said at the meeting. Generally there are two types of minutes:

ACTIVITY 5

Exercise

Some of the following terms appear in the chapter and some in the glossary on pages 200–204. Without looking at either, try to give a brief definition of:

(a) agenda;
(b) quorum;
(c) *ex officio* member;
(d) resolution;
(e) substantive motion;
(f) abstention.

Check your own definitions against the glossary and the text.

Flow chart of procedure for motions

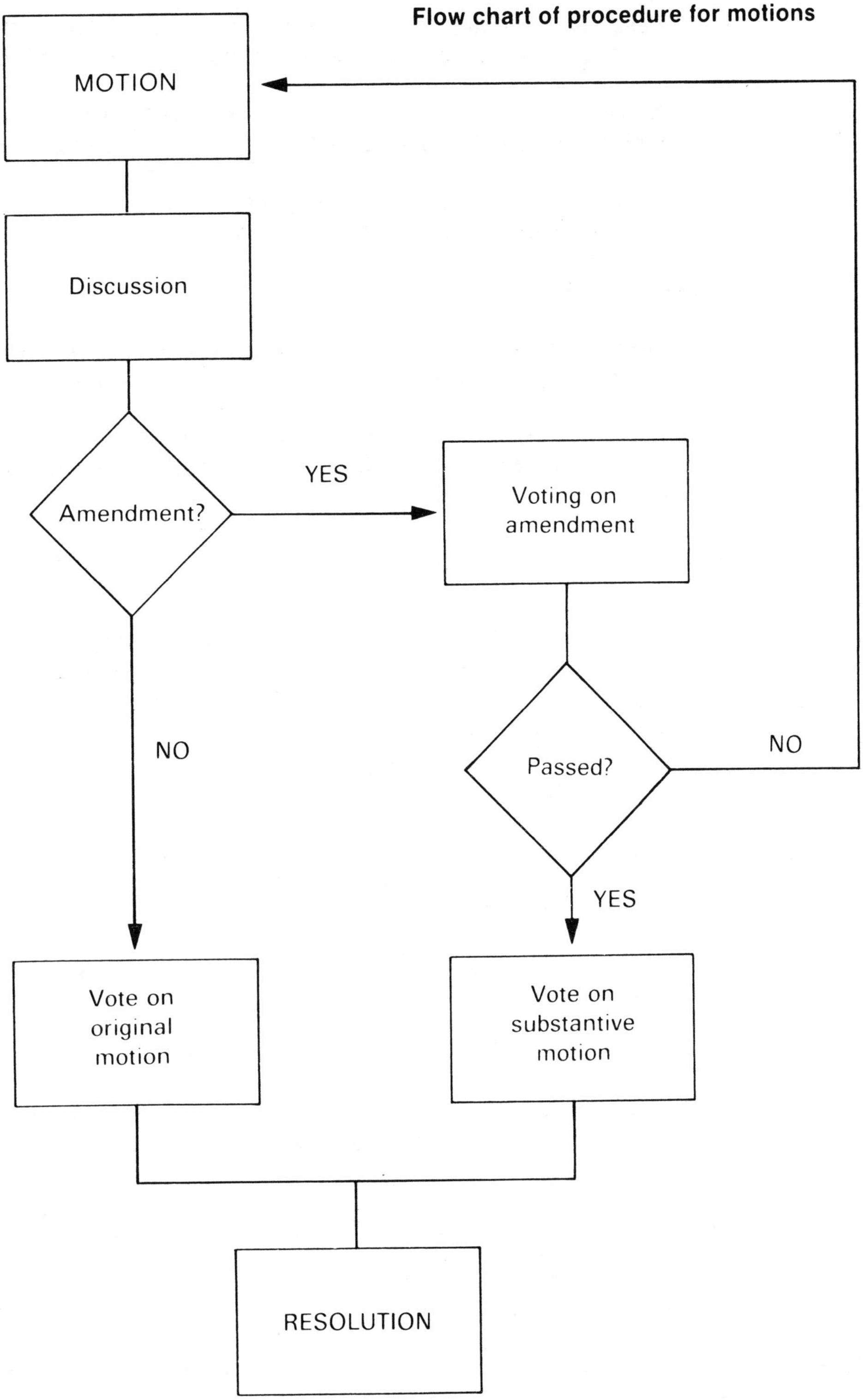

(a) *Resolution minutes* these only record very brief details and concentrate on the actual resolutions passed and the vote (see pages 187–188).

(b) *Narrative minutes* these include some details of the discussions which took place as well as the resolution and votes (see pages 185–186).

It is important that the right kind of minutes are used for any particular meeting. The advantages of each kind are listed below.

Narrative minutes

- If absent members want to check up on the exact nature of the discussion that took place in their absence, then these minutes may be preferable.

- If the chairperson wants to maintain some kind of profile of individual member's attitudes and standpoints on various issues these minutes may be useful.

- In the case of social/sport/other voluntary committees it may help members to feel that their contributions to the proceedings are valued.

- In the case of some 'political' committees, i.e. those which involve the members in impressing other people, narrative minutes can be used to convince them that the individual who speaks (and is noted/minuted) is powerful or important.

Resolution minutes

- This type of minute reinforces the idea that the resolution is a collective decision by which all members will stand, regardless of the debate which may have preceded it.

- It may be preferred by meetings that like short, succinct records rather than rambling reports.

Taking notes for minutes

If you are ever responsible for taking down the minutes at a formal meeting, the following guidelines should help to ensure that your notes are accurate and relevant:

- Record date, time and place of meeting.

- Make a list of all the members attending the meeting giving officials first and then an alphabetical list of members.

Example of narrative minutes

NATIONAL EASTERN BANK PLC

Minutes of the meeting of the Southern Region Social and Sports Association: Tuesday 7 May 19..

Present:	L.R. Allen	Kirkham Branch	
	Miss P.M. Cody	Shipton Branch	
	T.L. George	Finchester Branch	(Chairman)
	Mrs K.S. Hennessey	Pickford Branch	
	S.M. Moore	Cawsham Branch	
	M.P. Newman	Porthampton Branch	(Secretary)
	Mrs S.L. Ogilvy	Merton Branch	(Treasurer)
	L.R Yates	Newtown Branch	
	Miss B.L. Young	Ockingham Branch	(Secretary Social Sub-committee)
	P.S. Zacheray	Purdington Branch	(Chairman Social Sub-committee)

1. Apologies for absence: these were received from Mrs M.R. Keith of the Burbridge Branch and M.P. Evans of the Lowton Branch; they were both on holiday.

2. Minutes: as these had already been circulated, the Chairman asked if these could be taken as read and agreed as correct. It was unanimously resolved that they should be accepted, and they were signed by the Chairman.

3. Matters arising: there were no matters arising from the minutes of the last meeting.

4. Correspondence: the Secretary reported that correspondence had now been received confirming cricket and tennis fixtures for June to September. He circulated a list of these to the members to post in their branches and agreed to post copies to Burbridge and Lowton branches.

5. Treasurer's Report: this was brief, and had been circulated to all members in advance. There were no questions raised and it was unanimously resolved by members that this should be accepted.

6. Social Subcommittee's Report: Arrangements for July Ball: the Chairman of the Subcommittee reported that:

- the date had been confirmed as Saturday 29 July 19..,
- the venue had now been agreed as Finchester Leisure Centre,
- tickets would be ready within a week,
- catering arrangements were complete,
- a live band and a disco had been hired,
- publicity was already posted,
- branches would be circularised within the next few days.

There were no outstanding problems and the members agreed that the situation was now satisfactory.

7. The motion 'that a reduced membership fee should be charged to members under 18' proposed Miss B.L. Young (Ockingham Branch); seconded Mr L.R. Yates (Newtown Branch): Mr Yates stated that the present fee of £15 per annum was rather high for those on the lowest grades. After some discussion as to the amount of fee reduction an amendment was proposed by Mrs K.S. Hennessey that members under 18 should pay £10 p.a.; this was seconded by Miss P. Cody, and was passed nem. con. There were 3 abstentions. The substantive motion was then resolved unanimously.

8. Any Other Business: there was no other business.

9. Date of next meeting: this was agreed as 8 June 19.. at 7.30 p.m. The venue was to be the Porthampton Sports Centre. The Chairman then closed the meeting.

Signed:......................
Chairman

Example of resolution minutes

NATIONAL EASTERN BANK PLC

Minutes of the meeting of the Southern Region Social and Sports Association: Tuesday 7 May 19--

Present:			
	L.R. Allen	Kirkham Branch	
	Miss P.M. Cody	Shipton Branch	
	T.L. George	Finchester Branch	(Chairman)
	Mrs K.S. Hennessey	Pickford Branch	
	S.M. Moore	Cawsham Branch	
	M.P. Newman	Porthampton Branch	(Secretary)
	Mrs S.L. Ogilvy	Merton Branch	(Treasurer)
	L.R. Yates	Newtown Branch	
	Miss B.L. Young	Ockingham Branch	(Secretary Social Sub-committee)
	P.S. Zacheray	Purdington Branch	(Chairman Social Sub-committee)

---

1. Apologies for absence: received from Mrs M.R. Keith (Burbridge Branch) and M.P. Evans (Lowton Branch): on holiday.

2. Minutes: circulated in advance.
   RESOLVED: that the minutes were accepted; signed by Chairman.

3. Matters arising: none raised.

4. Correspondence: Secretary had confirmed cricket and tennis fixtures for June-September. List circulated to representatives for posting in branches, and copies to be posted to Burbridge and Lowton branches.

5. Treasurer's Report: circulated in advance.
   RESOLVED: that the report was accepted (unanimous).

6. Social Subcommittee's Report: Arrangements for July Ball
   - date: Saturday 29 July 19--
   - venue: Finchester Leisure Centre
   - tickets: ready within a week
   - catering arrangements: completed
   - music: live band and disco hired

- publicity: already posted; branches to be circularised in next few days.
  AGREED: no problems outstanding; arrangements satisfactory.

7. The motion 'that a reduced membership fee should be charged to members under 18' proposed Miss B.L. Young (Ockingham Branch); seconded Mr L.R. Yates (Newtown Branch). Discussion concerning amount led to amendment: 'that members under 18 should pay £10 p.a.': proposed Mrs K.S. Hennessey, seconded Miss P.M. Cody.
   RESOLVED: the substantive motion (unanimous)

8. Any Other Business: None

9. Date of next meeting: 8 June 19-- at 7.30 p.m.
   Venue: Porthampton Sports Centre.

Meeting closed.

Signed..................

Chairman

- Make a list of any apologies for absence together with any reasons given.

- Using the agenda as your guide, give each topic a clear subheading and briefly summarise the discussion (if narrative minutes) or the resolution (if resolution minutes). You need to record the decision taken, the votes counted, the action to be taken and by whom.

- Do not attempt to take down notes of every word spoken (this could, in fact, lead to legal action when members insult one another!). You need a *summary* of the *main* facts and arguments. Here, listening skills and practised note-taking, discussed earlier, can help you.

- Make maximum use of schematic note layout using capitals for headings, spacing and indentation. Use a referencing system of numbers or letters to identify clearly each heading, subheading and points.

- Where you need to record narrative minutes, ensure that you have statements attributed to the right person. *Always note* action to be taken by individual members.

- If you are uncertain about any points to be recorded you should ask the chairperson at the time—not leave it till later. Likewise, if the pace of the meeting prevents you from noting all the main points, then ask members to slow down or to repeat points.

- Never record *opinion* unless strictly relevant to the resolution (in the case of narrative minutes). Never write your notes from a personal point of view—you need an *objective* record.

Once you leave the meeting, try to draft the formal minutes as soon as possible. You should try to check your notes taken during the meeting against those recorded by the chairperson to make sure you agree on the discussion and the resolutions. The minutes, once produced, should be circulated to the members who attended, absent members and anyone who may be affected by the resolutions or who is required to take some form of action.

Agreeing Minutes Once the minutes have been circulated, members have the opportunity to read them. At the following meeting, the chairperson must ask if this has been done and/or read them out—though this is not usually necessary. What *is* essential is that he/she asks the members to agree them as an accurate record before he/she signs them as being correct. Once he/she does so, they are a *legal* record, and cannot be altered except by someone bringing a new motion to do so, which is then voted on by the entire committee.

Recording Minutes Only when minutes have been agreed are they entered in the minutes book (if there is one) or kept on file. They are vital in that they provide a permanent record for new and existing members on what actually occurred and was decided—people's memories are notoriously unreliable!

Of course, early in your career, you are much more likely to have to attend *informal* meetings—certainly on a more regular basis. They are the routine method by which information is broadcast or decisions taken. The last part of this chapter, therefore, is concerned with the purpose, conduct and control of these, since they happen far more frequently in the general routine of any financial institution.

INFORMAL MEETINGS

Informal meetings do not require all the strict formalities identified above. However, basic principles still apply. For instance, although there is no formal notice of meeting and agenda, people who are to attend an informal meeting still need to be invited or requested to come along by the person who has decided to call the meeting and it is also a good idea if they know in advance the general purpose of the meeting and what is to be discussed.

In the case of a more informal meeting at work, let's say within your work section, your boss is likely to request you to attend a meeting by word of mouth or by telephone. He/she will still have to tell you when and where it is to take place, what you will be discussing and any information he/she wants you to bring along. Even where the decision to meet is collective, e.g. a group of friends deciding to meet to go out for the evening, you still need to ensure that everyone concerned has the basic information of when, where and what.

Leadership

In formal meetings there is a person appointed or elected to control the meeting, i.e. the chairperson. In some informal meetings, we may still talk of someone chairing or leading the meeting. At departmental or section meetings, this is likely to be the person who has the greatest authority, or the person who may be responsible ultimately for solving a given problem or making a particular decision. However, in other situations a meeting may be a real encounter of equals and there is no obvious person to control the proceedings. You will find that a leaderless group does not function very easily and that all group situations eventually need someone to take a leadership role.

ACTIVITY 6

Pause for Thought

Think back to the last meeting you had with other people in which there was no obvious *appointed* leader, that is, you were all roughly on the same level of authority. Which member of the group emerged as the leader? Why do you think that person became leader of the group?

Now consider other informal leaderless meetings in which you have participated, e.g. a holiday group, an attempt to form a new social/sports group, your colleagues on a training course. Did the leaders who emerged in these situations have any personal characteristics in common with the person you have identified above, or were there some which were markedly different?

It is likely that in the above activity, you found that different groups needed different types of people to be leader and there is no consistent set of personality characteristics that make up leadership. Leadership is a role which is performed within a group and it is the specific group membership and the tasks the group is involved with that will determine who assumes the role. However, all leaders do have the following in common:

- They provide a focus for the group so that the group can structure its communication and activities in some way.
- They coordinate and harmonise what is happening within the group.
- They provide a motivational force.

To do this they probably have to be able to:

- **L**isten—to be attentive to what each person is saying.
- **E**mploy tact—to be firm but careful in handling members, and to be sensitive in responding to the mood of the meeting.
- **A**ssert themselves—to be able to control and direct proceedings.
- **D**ecide—to be able to make decisions to maintain and summarise progress, and manage decision-making.
- **E**xpress clearly—to be able to articulate ideas and feelings clearly and succinctly.

- **R**eact impartially—to show no favouritism or bias, and to be able to moderate or change decisions without self-pride.

In such informal groups the leader is the person whose personality enables him/her to help the rest of the group get on with the task in hand, satisfies the individual needs of the members, and represents the collective identity of the whole group—no mean task! Effective group leadership is often represented by the diagram below.

Characteristics of effective team leadership: keeping the balance

To identify the differences between chairing a formal meeting and *leading* an informal meeting, you may find the following helpful. However, it should be noted that these simplify the distinction, and the position of, for instance, a manager calling a meeting of his subordinates may have some of the characteristics of chairing rather than leading.

Chairing

- Rules and procedures govern the actions of the chairperson.
- The chairperson may not be free to respond to situations in the way he/she would like, since formal procedures may constrain such responses.
- Chairperson is normally appointed or elected before the meeting takes place and has the opportunity to prepare.
- There are specific procedures to remove the chairperson from office.

- ▶ Chairperson has *authority* to demand implementation of a decision.
- ▶ Whole atmosphere and environment of the meeting reinforces formality and the authority of the chairperson.

Leading

- ▶ Group codes of conduct developed over time; custom and practice may decide acceptable actions by leader.
- ▶ Leader has much more freedom to respond according to the needs of specific group situations and members.
- ▶ Leader may be decided in advance but leadership role *may* emerge during the group meeting, thus limiting the opportunity to prepare.
- ▶ Leader may lose role if he/she is ineffective or becomes unpopular.
- ▶ Leader has to use *persuasive powers* but not authority to implement decisions.
- ▶ The much more relaxed atmosphere reinforces a sense of equality and informality between members and the leader needs to use his/her personality to maintain control.

Some meetings, especially at work, demand both sets of characteristics in a situation which is informal but is called by someone who has the formal status to call and control a meeting for work purposes. These are often called *command meetings*.

Command Meetings

In your first few years at work, you are more likely to attend these than any other type. They combine characteristics of the formally chaired and the informally led meeting.

They are normally called by someone in a mangement position to discuss matters of concern, to monitor progress or to brief subordinates. Because of this, there is an appointed leader whose position in the organisation gives him/her authority to call and control the meeting. However, the fact that this person is calling a meeting indicates that he/she needs to communicate or ask for cooperation and therefore needs to employ powers of persuasion and self-presentation rather than rely on formal authority alone.

Even a formal chairperson needs to have some of the qualities implied here, so we can now look at the whole question of group working and group leadership.

GROUP WORKING AND MEETINGS

Whether you are chairperson/leader or a participant in a formal or informal meeting, to make the proceedings really effective, you not only need to know the rules, you also need to know something about human behaviour in group situations.

Meetings bring together people with a wide range of personalities, attitudes and motivations. Each person in a meeting, because of his/her unique characteristics, will interpret situations slightly differently. As a participant yourself, you will need to recognise each person's individuality, the motivation behind his/her behaviour and to use positive strategies for responding to the other group members. Very often we tend to notice the way in which other people hinder activities within a group—and then complain about them. We also have a tendency to stereotype (or typecast) individuals. In the illustration below we have caricatured types of group members.

ACTIVITY 7
Exercise

Look at the illustration above. Do any of these characters seem familiar to you?

What problems do each of these types present in a meeting? Write down some notes on these problems and then compare your notes with our list of suggestions at the end of this chapter.

The illustration may show caricatures but they also represent very real people. One of them may be you! Our behaviour at a meeting may be conditioned by a number of circumstances and by our feelings towards other people in the room. We can all *appear* to change character when we meet different situations. You only have to think of shy, retiring individuals who become raging, intolerant maniacs when they get behind the wheel of a car! You may appear quite different in an informal meeting with people who are your equals from how you appear in a meeting where your boss is present. We change our approach, our style of behaviour and even our vocabulary to suit particular circumstances. What is certain is that all of us exhibit positive and negative qualities in a group situation. Consider, for example, the notes in the table below.

Positive and negative characteristics of group members

Type	*Positive*	*Negative*
Persistent/quarrelsome/ habitual objector	Ensures point of view is heard; can play devil's advocate	Disruptive, can impede progress and stifle other people's contribution
Thick-skinned/know-all/ instant expert	*May* be useful source of information; can be relied on to contribute	Stifles other people's views; may *not* have real expertise; may quote irrelevant facts and figures
Dominant	Can provide a strong lead and provide unity	Over-bearing, opposed with difficulty; may cause others to withdraw
Silent	Can have positive effect if silent at appropriate times, i.e. not drawn into argument	Will not contribute facts or ideas and therefore makes no positive contribution; however, silence may be unnerving to others
Talkative	May act as ice-breaker; may stimulate others	If talks all through the meeting, becomes disruptive, time-wasting and boring
Performer/comedian	Relieves tension; may act as scapegoat for group	May not be listened to when making a serious contribution; may trivialise proceedings

Initiator	Helps meeting to progress by providing stimulation; will suggest solutions to problems; will volunteer original ideas	May produce ideas which are irrelevant or impracticable; may be more concerned with creating ideas than reaching decisions
Team leader/interpreter/ committee type	Can organise group; gives confidence to less experienced members; can express ideas in form that others can understand; participates actively and supports the group	Can relate more to the group than the purpose; may be more concerned with quoting rules and procedures than achieving progress
Supportive/mediator	Useful when supports purpose of meeting by providing additional facts or backing positive ideas; can take heat out of an argument so that discussion can progress by making efforts to achieve harmony	If support is for people rather than purpose, it can result in cliques; may want to appease everyone and won't risk giving offence; stifles useful discussion

Different qualities may be required in different circumstances. For instance, if you are in a meeting where your boss is giving out information or giving instructions to the group, you will need to play a relatively passive role and only ask questions when relevant. However, if you are part of a problem-solving meeting, everyone's ideas count and members will be expected to participate actively. Despite the fact that we do adapt our behaviour according to circumstances, you should recognise the fact that we do sometimes find it difficult to change in just the right way. If a person is by nature shy and retiring, they may find it very difficult suddenly to be active, forthright and outgoing if the meeting situation changes. Similarly the friendly, joking, outgoing type may find it difficult to stop talking and playing the fool when the situation demands.

However, the purpose of any meeting is to bring a number of people together to reach some joint decision or take some joint action and therefore, whatever the difficulties, the group must try to use each other's abilities positively.

ACTIVITY 8

Exercise

Go back to the illustration on page 194. For each character in turn think of at least one strategy that you can employ to use him/her in a positive way. You may find this activity easier if you imagine yourself as the group leader.

This is likely to be more problematic than the previous exercise.

Again, check your notes against our suggestions at the end of the chapter.

You may then like to decide for yourself whether you are one of the characters in the illustration or a completely different type. If so—who are you?

ALTERNATIVES TO FACE-TO-FACE MEETINGS

Today there are a number of alternatives to face-to-face meetings which busy executives may wish to choose.

Audio and Teleconferencing

These may be alternatives to face-to-face meetings particularly where long distances are involved. Busy managers in different regional areas (or international locations) can take part in audio conferencing by means of a telephone network link. Of course this will require particular attention to the telephone skills mentioned earlier in the book.

Teleconferencing (BT's facility is known as Confravision) involves using TV cameras and audio equipment to enable pictures and voice to be transmitted from one location to another via telecommunication networks (landlines, radio waves or satellite systems). This can be done by participants visiting a local studio of one of the large telecommunications companies or by the company setting up an "in-house" studio on the participant's premises. This is an expensive facility but it can be cheaper in time and money than bankers from different parts of the world having to come together in one place.

Since participants are still in a face-to-face situation, they will need to employ the speaking and listening skills mentioned in Chapters 1 and 2 of this book as well as the aspects relating to group working mentioned earlier in this chapter.

Computer Conferencing

Computer systems are available that enable a personal computer user to dial a colleague in another part of the world and, once their PCs are linked, to transmit a software application, e.g. a chart or document which can then be updated, modified or altered by the other person while they talk over the telephone.

CONCLUSION

Meetings are probably the most well used and the most ill used method of communication. This is largely because they employ oral methods and involve more than two people; all the communication barriers and problems are therefore present. Such problems can be minimised and even avoided, however, by good planning, preparation and participation. The principles discussed in this chapter should help you to become aware of some of the problems and give some guidance on how to overcome them. However, there is nothing so valuable as observation and experience—so watch carefully next time you attend any kind of meeting and critically evaluate the processes you observe, and, of course, your own performance.

SUGGESTED ANSWERS TO ACTIVITIES

Activity 3

Meeting	*Purpose*
Briefing by superior	To give instructions
Employer/trade union or staff association	To discuss matters of common interest to both parties or to conduct formal negotiations
Problem solving	To identify nature of the problem, to discuss alternatives to solving the problem and propose a course of action
Directors	To discuss and decide upon the policy for their company
Social committee	To discuss and make decisions relating to the terms of reference of the committee

Activity 7

1 Griffin This is the supportive type or mediator. Often regarded as a positive role, but can be a problem if anxiety not to give offence or to have an argument limits open discussion.

2 Horse This type initiates ideas and contributes information. This is not often a problem but can become so if he/she produces ideas that the others do not want to accept or cannot understand.

3 Monkey This is the talkative type, who constantly wants to monopolise the conversation, even when he/she has nothing relevant to say.

4 Frog This is the comedian or performer who may attempt to focus the attention of the group on him/herself by being funny or silly, or may use humour to trivialise the proceedings.

5 Fawn This is the shy type who is reluctant to make a contribution.

6 Hedgehog This is the supercilious or silent type who may withdraw from the proceedings and/or pour scorn on the contributions of others.

7 Hippo This thick-skinned type won't accept arguments of other people; always consider he/she is right.

8 Giraffe This type is over-dominant, powerful, and is opposed with difficulty.

9 Ant Eater This persistent type worries at a problem and may hold up proceedings because he/she must have answers to all queries.

10 And you the leader This is the team leader type and again tends to be a positive role. However, this type can be a problem if this individual is more anxious to be popular with the group than to achieve the task.

Activity 8

1 Griffin Use these qualities when harmony is necessary or when you need a mediator to bring two opposing parties together.

2 Horse Appeal to this type when ideas are going round in circles or the meeting falls silent. Stimulate his/her ideas with a direct question.

3 Monkey Interrupt his/her flow of words tactfully; limit speaking time.

4 Frog Use humour when tension needs to be relieved. Intercept quickly if acting becomes a distraction from the task.

5 *Fawn* Try to give reassurance and indicate that a contribution would be welcomed by the group.

6 *Hedgehog* Recognise any relevant knowledge or experience; ask directly for a contribution.

7 *Hippo* His/her ideas must be fully discussed by the group; must not be allowed to 'bulldoze' and force ideas on others. Keep referring ideas to the group.

8 *Giraffe* Assertive personality makes effect on the group similar to bulldog. Again, he/she must not be allowed to be over-assertive and other less forceful members should be asked for their ideas.

9 *Ant Eater* Open up objections or queries to the whole group so that they are fully discussed and resolved together.

GLOSSARY OF TERMS

Types of Meetings

ad hoc committee	Sometimes called a special, or special purpose committee. It will be appointed to deal with one particular issue.
advisory/consultative committee	A committee which refers advice to a main executive committee.
annual general meeting	A meeting of all the members of an organisation or shareholders of a company that must be held each year.
executive committee	A committee which has the authority to act on its decisions.
extraordinary general meeting	A meeting of all members of an organisation or shareholders of a company to discuss some matter of importance for which the consent of all or the majority of members is necessary.
standing committee	One which has no finite time-span but meets regularly during this indefinite period.
subcommittee	A group appointed by a main committee to undertake specified work on its behalf. It must report to the main committee periodically.

Documents

agenda	A list of items to be discussed at a meeting.
attendance record	The book in which each member present at a meeting signs his/her name.
chairperson's agenda	The agenda prepared for use by the chairperson.
constitution	The document which states the rules and procedures which govern the conduct of the meeting.
memorandum	A document setting out information to enable a committee to make a policy decision.
minute book	A book containing a signed copy of each set of minutes.
narrative minutes	A summary of all the points raised in discussion together with resolutions and votes.
resolution minutes	A summary of all the resolutions passed.
notice of meeting	A notification to members of the time, date and place of a meeting.

Conduct of Meeting

addendum	An amendment which *adds* words to a motion.
addressing the chair	A member wishing to speak on a point must rise and address the chairperson saying, 'Mr/Madam Chairman. . .'.
adjournment	The chairperson may, with the consent of the members, adjourn the meeting in order to postpone further discussion or because of shortage of time.
adjourned by consent	This means that the unfinished business of one meeting will be discussed at another meeting by consent of those present.
adjournment *sine die*	The unfinished business will be discussed at a future meeting but no date has been specified.

co-option	The power given to a committee to allow others to serve on the committee.
ex officio	Membership of a committee 'by virtue of one's office'.
intra vires	This means that the topic is within the powers of the person or committee concerned.
lie on the table	A matter is said to 'lie on the table' when no action can be taken on it.
motion	A proposal that certain action be taken.
next business	A motion 'that the meeting proceed with next business' is a method of delaying the decision on any matter brought before the meeting.
no confidence	When the members of a meeting disagree with the chairperson they may pass a vote of 'no confidence' in the chair. In this situation the chairperson must vacate the chair in favour of the vice-chairperson or some other person. There must be a substantial majority in favour of this motion.
point of order	A question regarding the procedure of a meeting or a query relating to the standing orders or constitution.
postponement	The action taken to defer a meeting to a later date.
proceedings	The business discussed, the main points of discussion and the decisions and agreements taken at a meeting.
proposer	The person who recommends a particular motion.
putting a question	To conclude the discussion on a motion it is usual for the chairperson to 'put the question' by announcing 'The question before the meeting is . . .'.
quorum	The minimum number of members necessary for a meeting to be held.

reference back	This is an amendment referring a report or other item of business back for further consideration to the body or person submitting it.
resolution	A formal decision carried by a meeting. A resolution cannot be cancelled (rescinded) at the meeting at which it was adopted.
rider	An additional clause or sentence added to a resolution after it has been passed. It differs from an amendment in that it adds to a resolution instead of altering it. It has to be proposed, seconded and put to the meeting in the same way as a motion.
right of reply	The proposer of a motion has the right to reply when the resolution has been fully discussed.
seconder	A person who supports the proposer of a motion.
standing orders	These are the rules compiled by the organisation to regulate the manner in which its business is conducted. May be called the 'constitution'.
substantive motion	A motion altered by a previously agreed amendment.
take the chair	This means that someone does the work of a chairperson during the meeting.
terms of reference	A statement of the work to be done by a committee.
ultra vires	When a matter is *ultra vires* it is outside the power or authority of the committee/organisation.

Voting

abstention	Where a member refrains from casting a vote either in favour or against a motion.
ballot	A written vote which preserves the secrecy of each individual's vote.
casting vote	An additional vote, usually held by the chairperson to enable a decision to be taken in the case of an equal number of votes being given for and against a motion.

going into division	The physical division of members for voting purposes.
majority	The greatest number of members either for or against a motion. The rules will define the majority of votes required to carry a motion.
nem. con.	(*Nemine contradicente*) The passing of a resolution without opposing votes but with some members abstaining.
nem. dis.	(*Nemine dissentiente*) Sometimes used instead of *nem. con.*
poll	This is the term used for the method of voting at an election. In a meeting this usually takes the form of a secret vote by ballot paper. The way a poll is conducted is usually laid down in the constitution.
proxy	A person authorised by a member to vote on his/her behalf.
scrutineer	The person who counts and examines closely the vote at an election.
teller	The person appointed to count the votes at a meeting.
unanimous	When all members of a meeting have voted in favour of a motion, it is said to be carried unanimously.
vote	To express, either verbally or in writing, whether one is for or against a motion.

Postscript

We hope that this book has increased your awareness of some of the problems in communication and given you some assistance in dealing with other members of the bank and with the public.

As your career progresses, you will have many opportunities to practise your communication skills and to improve them—although improvement can only occur if you are prepared to evaluate your own strengths and weaknesses realistically and to accept feedback from others. The truth usually lies somewhere between your own perception and that of others. In any case, we all need to ask the question 'How could I have communicated more successfully in this situation?' if we are to progress and develop. This is a lifelong process.

In the short term, however, and in the early stages of your career you progress by qualification. This book has been specifically designed to help you with the various communication methods which are assessed and valued by the Chartered Institute of Bankers. Further help on examination techniques is given in Supplement 1.

One area which may be a problem remains: that of English usage. The standards of candidates' written English are consistently criticised by examiners and employers; this is partly because the current education system often stresses other qualities at the cost of the basic building blocks of the English language. In Supplement 2 we have attempted to provide a quick and simple guide to some basic rules of sentence construction, punctuation and spelling—all traps for the unwary candidate! We hope that these prove useful to those who feel that they need some assistance in these aspects of English usage.

To conclude: poor communication damages your own reputation and image as well as that of your organisation. Effective communication, on the other hand, can be an extremely rewarding activity—in all senses of the word—for everyone concerned.

We wish you every success!

Supplement 1
Examination Techniques

Taking a Preliminary Certificate will not, of course, be your first experience of examinations; however, from examiners' reports and from discussions with candidates it would seem that there are a number of common problems which arise fairly constantly. This supplement is therefore included to give you some help in preparing for and taking the Certificate; the main points to remember are listed below—and they will, of course, be helpful in any examination situation.

PREPARATION

Finding out about the Paper

It is important to begin by finding out everything you can about the paper you are about to take. There are several ways you can do this, as follows:

(a) *Consult the syllabus* This is available from the Institute, and your tutor will certainly have a copy. Read this carefully and check any queries with your tutor. Remember that the syllabus will identify clearly the skills and abilities which the paper will set out to test; it is important for you to note these very carefully. In the case of the Preliminary Certificate, this will include correct presentation and content; it will *also* demand an ability to communicate effectively in correct, concise English. This is emphasised in the syllabus and in all guidance to candidates. Some help with English usage is therefore given in Supplement 2 and you should read this.

(b) *Consult past papers* These are available from the Institute and your tutor will also have copies. Later in this supplement we have included a specimen paper published by the Institute which has been annotated to help you. You can use past papers in the following ways:

(i) To check the *structure* of the paper, i.e. the number and type of questions to be answered. Although there may be minor changes from year to year, the main sections and the marks awarded for them are liable to remain similar.

(ii) To help you with *timing* your answers; you should *not assume* that you can answer certain types of questions in a given time—you need to try out some of the answers and test yourself. Time yourself strictly; this will give you valuable practice at working within time constraints. You could also try a whole 'mock' paper under the guidance of your tutor. You should preferably do all that is suggested here—the more you practise the better; you will also avoid unpleasant shocks on the day!

Revision

(a) *Timing your revision* Revision requires time management—it is far better to revise over a period of time so that you can consolidate your knowledge and practise your skills on example questions. You will find this far more effective than trying to cram a few rules into your head the night before. In this subject in particular, it is skills *development* rather than learning rules which is necessary. In any case, an examination tests your knowledge and skills under 'stress' conditions, so you need to be at your peak—not tired out from burning the midnight oil!

(b) *Revision methods* As we have suggested, practice on past papers can provide useful revision.

In addition, you might like to revise with a small group or with one other candidate. It helps to test one another and to 'pool' your good points so that you can both improve. Revising with others can also help to exert discipline; if you have met for the specific purpose of revising, it is likely that you will apply yourselves to the task; it can also provide motivation. At the very least revision is less boring in company!

Remember this is also your final opportunity to use your tutor's help. If you have any problems, you need to ask about them now; your tutor can also be very helpful in marking your practice answers and discussing them with you.

(c) *Examination nerves* Although preparation and revision can help to give you confidence and thus reduce stress levels, revising in a group also helps since everyone supports one another.

Remember that *some* nervousness is to be expected and it is not necessarily unhelpful—it stimulates you to give your best performance; any sportsperson will tell you this is true!

Otherwise, you may already know the best strategy to employ to reduce your own nervous tension. Every individual knows him or herself well enough to have learnt by experience how to cope. You now need to apply it to the exam situation. Some strategies include:

- relaxation exercises

- listening to music
- watching an absorbing programme or film
- chatting with a friend about matters unconnected with the examination

In any case, it is a good idea to try to have all your preparation complete so that you can take an evening off the night before—otherwise either staleness or tiredness can result.

ON THE DAY: TAKING THE EXAMINATION

(1) Ensure you have everything you need. A check-list is:

- your examination number, if you have one
- an accurate watch
- pens (more than one—this can run out!)
- pencils, ruler and compass for diagrams
- erasers (a rubber and liquid paper)

Whereas a few sweets to aid concentration and for refreshment are acceptable, a full-scale picnic is likely not to be.

(2) Arrive in plenty of time—at least 15 minutes before the examination starts. This helps you relax and also means that if there is a room change or you have to find the location, you have plenty of time. You need to avoid being rushed and flustered.

(3) Inform the invigilator if you need to take any medication (e.g. hay fever tablets) or have any medical condition of which he/she needs to be aware. Remember that invigilators are there to help—not just to watch you!

(4) Listen carefully to any specific instructions given by the invigilator and observe them. Make sure your watch is synchronised with the clock in the examination room or with the invigilator's watch—whichever is being used to time the examination.

(5) Read the whole paper before you pick up your pen. The consequence of not doing this is that you miss something vital. To illustrate this, read the paper below and decide what would happen if you had not carried out this preliminary reading!

READ ALL THE INSTRUCTIONS CAREFULLY BEFORE ANSWERING THE QUESTIONS

1. Write your name on the top right corner of this question paper
2. Draw two interlocking circles on the back of this paper, with a triangle on top of them
3. Fold the top left corner of this paper inwards by one inch
4. Shout your first name out loudly
5. Double underline your name at the top of the page
6. Draw a square around each number 5 that is on this paper
7. Shout out 'I am first in this test'
8. Cross out the first word in the first three questions
9. Ignore all instructions so far except instruction 1
10. Put your pen down

(6) Ensure that you know how many questions you must answer; do not waste time doing an unnecessary one because you have not read the instructions or because you want to impress the examiner. Your last answer will be disregarded if you do.

(7) If you have any doubts after your preliminary read through and after careful consideration of the instructions, query these immediately with the invigilator.

(8) Look at the weighting of marks given to each question; this should help you to determine the allocation of your time to each question. Some examination papers actually give suggested times; if they do this then do take advantage of the suggestions to guide you. If you know that you are rather slow or if you have difficulty with some subject areas, these indicators may also help you determine the order in which you undertake questions. It is obviously a good idea to ensure that you have sufficient time for the heavily weighted questions, so tackle these first.

(9) For some of the longer questions, particularly where layout and presentation are important or where reduction of words is necessary, you will need to prepare your answers by compiling some rough notes first. It is a good idea to write these in pencil and then cross them through with one line; if you do not finish your answer, the examiner can at least see what you intended to write.

(10) Try to leave enough time to check your answers at the end. Read through thoroughly and correct errors in English or content; insert any omissions and cross through any irrelevant or incorrect material. Check, too, that you have filled in the front of your examination book correctly, have numbered your questions clearly, have numbered your pages in correct sequence and that your paper is fastened securely together. It is safest to put your name on each sheet.

An annotated paper is included to help you further and this follows.

SPECIMEN EXAMINATION PAPER

Chartered Institute of Bankers
Stage 1

BANKING CERTIFICATE — PRELIMINARY SECTION

BUSINESS COMMUNICATIONS

18 May 1989

1. Read the instructions on the cover of the answer book.
2. **Answer ALL questions.** The number in brackets after each question, or part of a question, shows the marks allotted.
3. Candidates are reminded that orderly presentation and clear handwriting are essential in their answers.

1. Write about 400 words on ONE of the following—(a) or (b) or (c):

(a) Prepare a report, for submission to the appropriate committee of your local council, on the distribution of shops in your district. As a result of your survey the committee hopes to encourage other traders to come to the area if there is a need, or discourage further trade in some commodities. In addition to studying the availability of different kinds of merchandise, you may consider how the needs of various age-groups are met, and how many and varied are the large chain stores.

(b) You are asked to examine the provision in your place of work for the health and safety of all who use the premises. You should consider at least the following: measures for prevention and dealing with fire, first aid provision including the training of personnel, potential hazards, and means of access. You may also consider other aspects of a healthy environment. Your report is to be submitted to the manager and should include, where necesary, recommendations for improvement.

(c) **Either**
Your manager has asked for a report on the advantages and disadvantages to all concerned of opening High Street banks on Saturday mornings. Include in your report a consideration of the possible hours of opening and the types of business to be transacted.

Or
If you work in a bank that is already opening on Saturdays, prepare a progress report for your manager. Consider how well Saturday opening has been received by customers and staff, and make recommendations for further improvements. (30 marks)

2. The passage on the next two pages is an abridgement of an article in *Financial Times*, 28 March 1988. Suggest a title and present the substance of **lines 1—122 only** in note form, with headings, so that another person can follow it without difficulty. The number of words, including headings, should not exceed 200. (20 marks)

AN ARRAY of powerful technologies, exists today to help create "the store of tomorrow," yet retailers are showing a healthy reluctance to embrace too large a slice of the electronic future too rapidly.

The overriding impression is of an industry moving forward steadily but cautiously, testing each innovation carefully for benefit as it goes.

Innovation is being carried forward on three broad fronts: "electronic money", the "electronic shop window" and "the computer-integrated store".

Electronic money means, chiefly, electronic funds transfer at the point of sale (Eftpos) and the smart card.

Eftpos is a sleepy leopard whose spots have changed substantially over the past few years. Originally a technologist's dream involving the instantaneous movement of money from buyer to seller at the moment of sale, it has been refined over the years to match the business needs of banks and retailers, yet it still lacks charisma.

Dr Mandeville of the RMDP says research suggests that consumers are not so much hostile to Eftpos as apathetic. Mr Simon Brodie of Coopers & Lybrand agrees, arguing that in the UK "it lacks a champion and we are probably doomed to a multiplicity of solutions."

And that would seem to be true for Eftpos worldwide.

In the UK, however, while banks and building societies are pressing ahead with their own Eftpos trials, the focus of interest has become the progress of the national scheme now being implemented by EftPos UK, a company set up by 11 clearing banks and (so far) three building societies, to manage the scheme.

Brian Allison, EftPos UK managing director, says that developments are on schedule: "We are firing on every conceivable cylinder.

Already a number of banks have taken delivery of special software enabling them to connect into the national system.

According to Mr Allison, the inaugural service, designed to test every aspect of the national system, will now go live in the spring of 1989.

Major worries for all organisations developing electronic money transtransmission systems are the security and integrity of the transmission mechanism. The "smart card", developed in France, and promoted there and elsewhere as an electronic cheque book, offers one solution to the problem of less than perfect telecommunications systems.

Containing a complete microcomputer within dimensions no greater than those of a conventional credit card, the smart card can be "charged" with electronic credit which is depleted as the card is used. It can function, furthermore, without the need for a counter terminal connected online to a central computer. It has adequate computing power and memory to carry out calculations to prove it is a valid card and to record every transaction for which it is used.

The electronic shop window embraces all the various uses of video in retailing. Some are apparently quite trivial yet can have powerful marketing significance. The "magic mirror" for example, pioneered in the US and involving video techniques to display an image of the customer upon which can be superimposed clothes, jewellery, make-up and so on.

Teleshopping is another example. The idea of shopping by telephone after sifting through goods displayed on a television screen has always proved better in theory than in practice.

Now some see it as the "shopping machine" the logical replacement for today's mail-order systems dependent on "Nellie down the corridor" selling to her friends and relations.

The "computer integrated store" represents a high point in retail automation. It implies the use of electronic point of sales systems, coupled to the electronic transmission of trading documentation between retailers, wholesalers and manufacturers.

Epos, the computer in the cash till, connected to the computer in the store, connected — in turn — to the computer at headquarters, is very much the key to the whole process.

ICL, the UK-based mainframe computer manufacturer, which claims a leadership position in the UK Epos market has published figures suggesting that "the penetration of Epos equipment in the UK retail sector will be spectacular, with large and medium-sized retail organisations accounting for the bulk of this growth."

It suggests that the total population of 58,000 Epos terminals installed in 1986 will grow to 410,000 by 1993. All the major mainframe computer manufacturers — IBM, ICL, DEC, NCR and Unisys — are now offering equipment for retail automation.

Dr Mandeville of the RMDP has identified a trend among these vendors to provide "one-stop shopping" for their customers. Conventionally, retailers purchased a mainframe from one supplier, Epos systems from another, and the communications and software to put the whole system together from others.

The resulting confusion of sometimes incompatible equipment had a powerful effect in slowing down the speed with which systems were implemented. Now alliances are being formed between suppliers so that com-plete systems can be offered.

Such alliances should remove at least one of the retailers' last traditional objections to investing in technology. Indeed, in areas like Eftpos and Epos, they are today likely to be wholehearted converts with only the cost of the equipment and the evidence of return on investment standing between them and enthusiastic adoption.

On both counts, time and technology are on their side. The cost of retailing equipment seems set to fall dramatically with advances in semiconductors, especially on the memory side. Meanwhile, a growing body of evidence indicates that the retailer who does not stay technologically-aware will be condemned to the sidelines in an increasingly electronic marketplace.

3. Using the same passage from *Financial Times* answer the following questions:

(a) Each of the following words is followed by three others. In each case choose **ONE** which would be the best substitute in this passage.

(i)	charisma (line 26)	attractiveness, grace, inspiration.
(ii)	apathetic (line 30)	indifferent, lack-lustre, unsympathetic.
(iii)	integrity (line 61)	efficiency, reliability, safety.
(iv)	conventionally (line 133)	customarily, invariably, naturally.
(v)	incompatible (line 140)	incomparable, inferior, irreconcilable.

(*5 marks*)

(b) In your own words explain the two statements:

(i) 'Eftpos is a sleepy leopard whose spots have changed substantially over the past few years.' (lines 18-20) (*3 marks*)

(ii) 'We are firing on every conceivable cylinder.' (lines 48-49) (*3 marks*)

(c) In the provision of 'one-stop shopping' (line 132) who are the vendors and who are the customers? (*2 marks*)

(d) Which **TWO** factors have caused retailers to be cautious over investing in the new technology? (*2 marks*)

(*Total marks for question — 15*)

4. Write a letter on **ONE** of the following topics:

Either

(a) A customer to whom you have given much help recently in his financial affairs, but is not a personal friend, has written to you at your bank to congratulate you on your promotion to a post in another area. He also expresses his appreciation of the contribution you have made to social and charitable activities in the area. Write an appropriate letter of thanks, which refers to the items mentioned, and express your regrets on leaving the town and hopes for the future.

Or

(b) As secretary of a sports club you have received a letter of complaint from Mrs A. S. Knight whose house and garden adjoin your field. She says that she writes also on behalf of other residents who suffer during the summer from children climbing and breaking fences to retrieve balls.

You have a problem here as the children are not those of your members and are playing on the field without permission. You also have difficulties over people exercising their dogs, or damaging the turf with their golf clubs.

Write her a courteous letter pointing out the difficulties and offering to meet the residents to discuss ways of dealing with these trespassers. (*15 marks*)

5. Set out a telephone message with all the usual headings and details, and expand the following words efficiently so that there will be no misunderstanding:

   "Helen, your meeting is postponed till next week. Please let the other two know." (*10 marks*)

6. Answer **ALL** the following questions, which relate to formal procedure at business meetings:

   (a) As chairman, what instructions would you give to two members who start arguing with each other? (*2 marks*)

   (b) What is meant by the chairman's 'casting vote' and when is it used? (*2 marks*)

   (c) Distinguish between a *motion* and a *resolution*. (*2 marks*)

   (d) What is meant by the minutes being 'taken as read'? (*2 marks*)

   (e) Place the following items of business in the commonly accepted order on an agenda:

   Correspondence, minutes, apologies, matters arising, A.O.B., main business. (*2 marks*)

   (*Total marks for question — 10*)

Reproduced by kind permission of the Chartered Institute of Bankers.

COMMENTS ON THE SPECIMEN EXAMINATION PAPER

1. Report

In the report question you are given a choice of subjects, sometimes of three, sometimes of two. The subjects vary but are normally either on an aspect of banking or on a general topic of social concern or on local business subjects. They are all likely to be related to your experience to date and have been set with young entrants to banks in mind.

You should spend about *one hour* on the report question. You will note that it usually carries 30 marks. These marks are likely to be allocated in the following way:

15 marks will be given to your choice of subject-matter, the way in which you organise that subject-matter in terms of paragraphing, order and layout.

15 marks will be given for how you express yourself in terms of your choice of words and phrases, the correctness of your sentence structures, your clarity and precision to the reader.

It is worth warning you that as much as 5 marks can be deducted for inaccuracies in the English language—for example, grammar, spelling and punctuation. Help for this question therefore is provided in Chapter 7 and Supplement 2.

2. Summary

You need to spend about 30-45 minutes on this question. Occasionally the summary will be required as a precis; more often you will be asked for a note form summary. It usually carries 20 or 25 marks which are likely to be allocated as follows:

- Use of headings in the case of a note form summary; these should be precise yet comprehensive; subheadings should be proper subheadings and not direct questions or journalistic headlines.

- Credit for selecting the essential details only, demonstrating that you have understood the passage and your ability to transfer that understanding to the reader.

The rest of the marks (15/20 in all) are awarded for *content* and are divided up according to the essential material in the passage. For example, if you refer back to Chapter 5, you will note that there are five major sections in the model answer given. It may be that 3 marks are awarded for each section or that slightly more proportionally may be given to section 4 which has more points included.

It is very important is that you identify the themes of the passage as a whole and ensure that these are stated in your introductory points—see sections 1(a) and 1(b) in the suggested answer on page 109.

3. Comprehension

You need to spend about *30 minutes* on this question—according to its length and the number of marks awarded. You will see that with this paper 15 marks are given but sometimes a shorter comprehension is given, for 10 marks, or a longer one, for 20 marks—so you will have to allocate your time accordingly.

Questions given relate to vocabulary, expression and, sometimes use of English. You will see that we have given some help with the vocabulary questions in Chapter 5.

Help for the note form summary and comprehension questions can be found in Chapter 5.

4. Letter

The subject of the letter is normally related to customer enquiry or complaints. You are given a choice of two letters and occasionally one letter may be of a general nature, for example, concerning a club or organisation to which you might belong.

You need to spend about *15 minutes* on this question. The 15 marks are allocated in the following way:

5 marks are given for the correct layout and formalities, as discussed in Chapter 3.

10 marks are given for adequate content and for the correct tone, observing the six C's of communication referred to throughout this book.

Again, note that 1 or 2 marks may be deducted for inaccuracies of grammar, spelling or punctuation.

Help for this question can be found in Chapter 3 and Supplement 2.

Questions 5 and 6

There are normally two final questions which deal with:

(a) the economic and efficient use of telephone or other telecommunications systems, particularly telegrams, telemessages and telex;

(b) the correct methods of conducting and controlling meetings and meetings terminology.

Sometimes these questions are phrased as short questions requiring brief answers or are set to be answered as a letter, memo or composed message.

The allocation of marks in this paper for the meetings question is usually 10. Help for the meetings question in whatever form it is set is given in Chapter 9 and you should familiarise yourself thoroughly with the correct form of documentation and terminology and the duties of officers.

Occasionally a memorandum is required in this question, so you should also be familiar with the correct layout and composition of memoranda, as discussed in Chapter 6.

The assignments we have set in this book should help you to cover the kinds of question likely to be set in the paper.

In addition your tutor should be able to refer to the examiner's reports from previous papers (provided by the Chartered Institute of Bankers) to give you more specific guidance on individual questions set each year — such as the one given in this supplement (May 1989).

Supplement 2 English Usage

In this supplement some guidance is given on the most important aspects of English usage; these are spelling, parts of speech, sentence and paragraph structure and punctuation. Correct usage is emphasised both in the syllabus and on the examination paper, since it is essential to correct communication. You may, however, use the supplement for reference purposes only—to look up a rule when you are unsure; you should also, of course, use a good dictionary.

INTRODUCTION

Any foreigner will tell you that English is a difficult language to learn; it's not easy even for the English! The reason is that English derives from a number of different origins—French, German, Latin, Greek, to name but a few. The result is a rich but often illogical language, as with our notoriously difficult spelling. How *do* you explain the different pronunciations of though, through, cough and bough, for example?

There are *some* rules, however, and it is wise to master these. There are also important lessons to be learned about the *construction* of English—words, sentences and paragraphs make up the basic *structure* of the language, and any individual must learn how to use these properly. Unfortunately, the fundamental skills have been neglected in the recent past, partly because of changing educational practices. The result is that employers—above all the banks—often complain about the lack of literacy in their young employees. A career in banking necessarily involves high standards in English if communication with customers and colleagues is to be successful. The Preliminary Certificate syllabus therefore rightly emphasises testing these skills in candidates.

This supplement has been included to assist those who have not had the required grounding in English usage; help is provided in the areas of spelling, sentence construction/parts of speech and punctuation.

SELF-CHECK QUESTIONS

You might like to check your knowledge of English usage by undertaking the following short exercises and checking your answers from the supplement.

SELF-CHECK TEST 1

Spelling Ability

Try to spell the following words by filling in the blank spaces (please note that the number of dots *does not* indicate the number of letters to be inserted).

	Definition
(1) ac......dation	housing or lodging
(2) bu....ness	commercial organisation
(3) co....tee	a formal meeting
(4) d...f..te	precise, firm
(5) emba......sed	confused, self-conscious
(6) fu...fi...	carry out an undertaking
(7) gr...ful	obliged, glad
(8) ind..p..nt	self-reliant, self-sufficient
(9) oc...red	happened
(10) prof....sion	an occupation requiring advanced qualifications

You can check your answers against the list in the spelling section on pages 225–6.

SELF-CHECK TEST 2

Parts of Speech and Sentence Structure

(1) Identify the nouns and pronouns in the following sentence; try to identify the *kind* of noun or pronoun:

> Carol is an employee on the full-time staff of the National Eastern Bank; it prefers to employ people like her, who think that good communication is important.

Check your answer against the nouns and pronouns sections on pages 228–9.

(2) Identify the adjectives and adverbs in the following sentences:

> Please type this letter quickly; it is urgent. Even though you are typing fast, you can still produce good copy.

Check your answers against the adjectives and adverbs sections on pages 229 and 232.

(3) Are the following sentences? If not, why not?

Referring to your letter.
Hoping to hear from you.

Check your answers against the information provided in section C on page 234.

(4) Identify the subject, verb and object in the following:

The customer signed the cheque.

Check your answer on page 235.

SELF-CHECK TEST 3

Punctuation

(1) If you wished to replace the word 'and' in the following sentence, what punctuation mark would you use?

She has worked very hard this year *and* it is not surprising that she has been promoted.

Check your answer in section (D) on page 239.

(2) In a letter, what punctuation mark is required after the following:

Would you be good enough to fill in the enclosed form

Check your answer in section (D) on page 238.

(3) Which 'its' needs an apostrophe?

(a) Its a nice day.
(b) The bank tries to give a good service to its customers.

Check your answer on page 240.

(4) Where would you put the colon and the commas in the following sentence?

The following items were ordered envelopes headed notepaper pencils and pens.

Check your answer on page 240.

If you were entirely accurate (without cheating) you already have a high standard of English usage and will only need to refer to the supplement in exceptional cases.

If you made a few errors, you have identified one or two areas which you need to refer to or study.

If your errors were frequent, you should take time to study the supplement in some detail and to check back with your tutor frequently on correct usage.

SECTION A SPELLING: THE RULES OF THE GAME
(and, of course, the exceptions!)

Let's begin with the perennial problem of spelling. There are a number of rules, and there are also identifiable problem words which are commonly misspelt or confused with others which sound similar to them. Perhaps it would be useful to look at a few basic rules which are easily followed, and of course at their exceptions. We have concentrated on vocabulary which is in daily use within the banks to explain these rules, so that you have a chance to apply and practise these immediately.

'I' before 'e' except after 'c'

For example, believe, relief but receive, receipt.

Everyone has heard of this rule, of course, and it is particularly important in banking where words like receipt are in constant use. There are exceptions, though—one important group is the words built on the word 'reign', e.g. 'sovereign', 'foreign', and one other common exception is 'seize'. Generally, the rule holds good.

Plurals

As you know the general rule is simply to add an 's', e.g. cheque, cheques. However, there are a few other rules which you should note carefully, as follows:

(a) *Words ending in 'y'* When this is preceded by a consonant, change the 'y' to 'i' and add 'es', e.g.:

company	companies
secretary	secretaries

(b) *Words ending in 's', 'ss'; 'sh', 'ch'; 'x' or 'z'* All these add 'es' in the plural, e.g.:

success	successes
match	matches
mix	mixes

(c) *The exceptions—irregular plurals* There are exceptions to all rules. Usually these derive from foreign words.

One important group which is extremely familiar is:

man	men
woman	women
child	children

Another is those words ending in 'f' which discard the 'f' for 'v' and add 'es':

hoof	hooves

There are others, however, and they really need to be learnt; some of the most common are listed below:

(i) Words ending in 'um' in the singular and which derive from Latin. These end in 'a' in the plural. They are also used in the business world, so they do need memorising.

memorandum	memoranda
addendum	addenda
medium	media

(ii) Similarly, some words of Latin derivation ending in 'a' in the singular, take 'ae' in the plural.

formula	formulae

(iii) Some ending in 'x' take 'ces' in the plural.

appendix	appendices

(v) Some ending in 'eau' add an 'x' in the plural.

bureau	bureaux

There is also one important group of words which always stay the same—they are already plural, so they do not take an 's'. Perhaps the most important of these—and they often cause confusion for overseas students—are:

information
staff

There are also some which are identical in the singular and plural (such as fish) but these do not usually enter into everyday banking terminology!

Prefixes

A prefix is an addition which *precedes* a word, often to give it a negative meaning. A very useful rule is that this does *not* alter the spelling of the original word. Some important examples are:

necessary	unnecessary
possible	impossible
probable	improbable

There are some prefixes which are followed by a hyphen, but the general rule above holds good, e.g.:

elect	re-elect

Other difficult beginnings There are a number of words which begin with silent (not pronounced) letters, such as 'know', and others which begin with 'ph' sounded as 'f'. Again, these usually derive from foreign words, in the last case from Greek. We have only listed here the most common and those most likely to cause confusion.

psychology (silent p)
physical (ph = f)
physiological (ph = f)
philosopher (ph = f)
knowledge (silent k)
knife (silent k)

Whereas these words are not usual in banking terminology, they are the most likely to appear in your general reading.

Suffixes

A suffix is an addition which *follows* a word and there are a number of different rules here.

(a) *Where 'ly' is added* (usually to make an adjective into an adverb—see page 232), the word itself does *not* change its spelling. Important examples—and those often causing problems—are:

sincere	sincerely
immediate	immediately
definite	definitely

This also holds true for words already ending in 'l', e.g.:

critical	critically
actual	actually
typical	typically

(b) *Where 'ness' is added* (usually to make an adjective into a noun—see page 228), the original word does *not* change either, except if the word ends in 'y' when this is usually replaced by 'i', e.g.:

useful	usefulness
happy	happiness

(c) *Where 'ing' is added*, usually this does not alter the original spelling of the word, as in bank, banking, but there are two important groups of exceptions here:

(i) When a word ends in 'e', the 'e' is dropped, e.g.:

write	writing
serve	serving

(ii) When a word ends in a consonant preceded by a vowel, that consonant is doubled before adding 'ing' (or 'ed')

stop	stopping	(stopped)
permit	permitting	(permitted)
refer	referring	(referred)
fulfil	fulfilling	(fulfilled)
occur	occurring	(occurred)

All these seem to cause confusion; it is worth noting them carefully—they are all words in constant use in business letters. There are, however, a number of exceptions involving banking terms. For example:

credit	crediting	(credited)
debit	debiting	(debited)

(d) There is a very confusing group, again deriving from Latin origins, where some words end in 'ible' and some in 'able'. There is no real rule here and they have to be learnt. If in doubt—look them up!

Words which Sound the same but are Spelt differently (Homophones)

There are too many of these to list, but it is worth noting some which give the most difficulty.

(a) One important group are those where the verb ends in 'se' but the noun in 'ce', e.g.:

to license	but	a (driving) licence
to practise	but	a (piano) practice
to advise	but	some (good) advice

(b) Among the most common errors are:

principle (standard)	principal (chief, main)
to affect (to change, to influence)	to effect (to put into practice)
stationery (paper, etc.)	stationary (at a standstill)
dependent (relying on)	a dependant (a *person* who is dependent)
draft (to draw up a document)	draught (a current of air)
complement (something which *completes* another)	compliment (a favourable comment)
council (a governing body)	counsel (advice)
sight (eye-sight)	a site (a location) to cite (to refer to)
whether (or not)	weather (climate) wether (a ram)

There are, of course, many more, but these are some of those most frequently misused. As always, if in doubt make use of a good dictionary.

And some last Words ...

Apart from the words quoted elsewhere in this section which are all in everyday use in business and are commonly misspelt, there follows a short list of others which give difficulty. You might like to add to your word power and learn these.

A	**B**	**C**
accommodation	beneficial	chargeable
acquire	benefit	committed
address	benefited	committee
advertisement	breadth	conscious
analysis	business	
argument		

D
deferment
deferred
definite
development

E
eligible
embarrass
environment
equipment
equipped
envelope

F
fulfil
fulfillment

G
gauge
grateful

H
height
honourable
honorary
humourous

I
illegible
inconsistent
independent
insistent
integrate
intellect
intelligible

J
judicial
judiciary
judge

K
knowledgeable

L
laborious
liaise
liaison
lose
loose

M
maintain
maintenance
manoeuvre
mischief
mischievous
miscellaneous

N
necessary
negligent
negligible
negotiate
notable
noticeable

O
occasion
occasionally
occur
occurred
omission
omitted

P
parallel
precede
proceed
procedure
profess
profession
prejudice
privilege
pursuit

Q
queue
query
quite
questionnaire

R
receive
recommend
referred
regrettable
resistant

S
separate
sincerely
skilful
skilfully
straight
succeed
supersede

T
technical
technological
temporary

U
unnecessary
unitary
urgency

V
valuing
valuable
various
verify
visible

W
whether
weather
wholly

X, Y, Z
yield

It is worth identifying the ones which you consistently spell wrongly, and really make an effort to eliminate your own mistakes—one of the problems is that we often ignore someone else's corrections! Make sure *you* do note corrections. As always, a good dictionary is an enormous help and you should always refer to one if you are doubtful about a spelling in your daily work. We can, after all, only help with the most usual errors here, but it is to be hoped that this part of the supplement has given some useful guidance on the complexities of English spelling.

SECTION B THE PARTS OF SPEECH: ESSENTIAL GRAMMAR

Being able to spell words accurately is important but recognising what each word *is* and what part it plays in the structure of a sentence is equally essential if you are to construct a sentence correctly. Again, this knowledge has been rather neglected in recent years, so it is useful to define briefly the roles played by each kind of word—what is known as the 'parts of speech'. The sentence is the framework of our speech, and it is important to know how the words fit into this correctly.

The main divisions in English are articles, nouns, pronouns, adjectives, verbs, adverbs, conjunctions and prepositions. For your guidance we will define each of these, and give some examples.

Articles

These are the most common words in the language: the, a an (before a vowel). 'The' is known as the *definite* article and the other two as *indefinite* articles, e.g. the bank, a deposit, an employee.

Nouns

Nouns are *names*—of objects, people or even ideas. They are subdivided into different groups:

(a) *Common nouns*—the names of everyday objects or concepts, e.g. pen, form, account, report.

(b) *Proper nouns*—the names of people, places, firms, etc., e.g. Carol, Paris, National Eastern Bank. Words in this group always begin with a capital letter.

(c) *Abstract nouns*—those which describe an idea, e.g. justice, communication, productivity.

(d) *Collective nouns*—words used for collections of people or things, e.g. team, staff, board, council. We have already dealt with the plural of nouns, some of which are irregular, on pages 221–3.

Pronouns

These are words which stand in place of a noun; they are often used to refer back to a noun so that we do not have to repeat it. For example we could write:

The bank is a financial institution. The bank employs many people.

However, this is neater if it is expressed as:

The bank is a financial institution. *It* employs many people. *Or*

The bank is a financial institution *which* employs many people.

Again, pronouns fall into a number of groups:

(a) Those which stand *instead of people*: for example, I, you, he, she, him, her, we us, they, them, or myself, yourself, himself, ourselves, themselves.

(b) Those which stand *in place of things*: it, them, that, this, those, these, e.g.:

He likes *them*, but I prefer *those*.

(c) Those which describe objects as *belonging to someone*: mine, ours, yours, theirs, e.g.:

These books are *mine*; those are *yours*.

NB These pronouns do *not* have an apostrophe (see pages 240–1).

(d) Pronouns which *introduce more information about a noun* as in the example above: The bank is a financial institution *which* employs many people.

(e) Pronouns which ask questions: who, to whom, what, etc., e.g.:

Who called this morning?
To whom did you give the report?
What is your name?

NB 'Who' is used when the pronoun is the *subject* of the sentence; 'whom' is used when it is the *object* or after a preposition—see page 235.

Adjectives

Adjectives describe a noun or a pronoun; they tell you something further about the person, object or idea concerned. Usually they come before the noun or pronoun they describe, but not always, e.g.:

This is the *pink* form, which is the one you need.
This form is *pink*.
This is an *urgent* letter.
This letter is *urgent*.

If there is more than one adjective, commas are used, e.g.:

The bank was large, modern, well-lit and very pleasant.

There are three other types of adjective, apart from the straightforward ones above:

(a) Those which show possession: my, your his, her its, our, their, e.g.:

This is *his* desk.
These are *their* accounts.
The bank tries to give a good service to *its* customers.

An important point to note in this last sentence is that when 'its' is used as an adjective it *never* has an apostrophe (see page 240). Only when 'its' is used as an abbreviation for 'it is' (e.g. It's a nice day) does it contain an apostrophe.

(b) Those which are used to emphasise or refer to a particular noun, e.g.:

This report is excellent; *that* one is very weak.

(c) Those which introduce a question: 'what' and 'which' can be used as adjectives in this way, e.g.:

What kind of account would you recommend?
Which brochure do I need?

Verbs

In English, the main strut on which each sentence rests is the verb. Verbs are often described as 'doing' words, but they can describe 'being' as well—states of mind, feelings or even existence. Consider the following examples:

The clerk *wrote* the letter.	('doing' word)
The clerk *was interested* in his job.	(a state of mind)
The clerk *was* John Hopper.	(a state of being)

The Active and Passive Verbs can be used in two ways (or 'moods' as they are sometimes called)—the active or the passive. The first is the more straightforward, and often more personal; the latter is sometimes used to distance the person concerned from what is happening—to make the message more impersonal. Typical examples are:

I *have noticed* that your account is overdrawn. (active)
It *has been drawn* to our attention that your account is overdrawn. (passive)

You may have drawn the conclusion—quite rightly—that the passive is often used to convey an unwelcome message! Generally, however, it tends to sound rather stilted and pompous.

Some Common Errors with Verbs

(a) *The dangling participle*—incomplete verbs: perhaps the most common error is what has been called the 'dangling participle'; unfortunately a very common mistake in business letters.

Look at the following:

Referring to your letter of 14th April. I can find no record of your standing order.
Referring to your letter of 14th April, I can find no record of your standing order.

The first is incorrect. 'Referring' is *not* a complete verb it is only a participle— a part of the verb. It would have to be, 'I am referring (or I refer) to your letter of the 14th April' to be complete, and only then should it be followed by a full stop. The second is acceptable because there is only a comma, which makes the whole phrase able to depend on the main verb 'can find'. So when you see an 'ing' apparently as the only part of a verb in a sentence, beware! It is probably incorrect. Other common examples are:

Incorrect	*Correct*
Hoping to hear from you.	I hope to hear from you.
Looking forward to your reply.	I look forward to your reply.

These tend to occur most frequently at the beginnings and endings of letters, so be particularly on your guard here.

(b) *Shall and will; should and would*—these are often muddled, and it is scarcely surprising. The rule is that in the first person singular or plural (I, we) *shall* simply expresses the future; but in the second and third person it shows intention or determination. Thus, 'I shall go' means simply that in the future; but 'I will go' means 'I am determined to go'. Conversely, 'He will go' means only that in the future, but 'he shall go' means that he must be made to go. The difference is summed up by the man who called out wrongly, 'I will drown; no one shall save me'! It's easy enough to see here but not as easy in daily use where we hear the two used interchangeably.

'Should' and 'would' follow the same rules in the future, but their usage is even more complicated. 'Should' is often used instead of 'ought to', e.g.:

He should be more careful.

Sometimes it is used as a conditional, usually paired with 'if', e.g.:

If this should happen again, he will have to leave.

'Would' can also be used to express an intention, but with a condition attached to it, e.g.:

I would go, if I were able to do so, but I have too much work.

(c) *May and might*—these also express an intention in which there is an element of uncertainty. They tend to be used interchangeably in this sense. Again, they are often followed or preceded by 'if' and therefore used in a conditional sense, e.g.:

If he arrives early, I might/may be able to meet him, but I have to leave at 8 o'clock.
I might/may be able to pass the examination, if I have revised well enough.

'May' is sometimes used in two different senses: one is 'to be permitted', as in:

You may go, if you wish; the manager has agreed.

(Note that *can* is *not* interchangeable with may—that would mean you were *able* to go, not that you had been *permitted* to do so.)

The other sense in which it may be used is to express *doubt*, e.g.:

Whatever that may be, it is not a report!

or, very rarely, *hope*, as in:

May the best man win!

May, might, shall, will, should and would are unfortunately so commonly used interchangeably that it is now difficult to lay down hard and fast rules. English is an organic, changing language and usage is often dictated by just that—how it is used (or even misused). It is hoped, however, that this may provide some guidance.

Adverbs

These give information about verbs, in the same way as adjectives describe nouns. They answer questions about the verb such as 'how', 'when' or 'where', e.g.:

She writes *quickly*, (answers *how* she writes).
He replied to that letter *recently*, (answers the question *when*).

Usually adverbs end in 'ly' but some irregular ones do not; two examples are 'fast' and 'late', e.g.:

He arrived late, even though he had driven fast, (late answers when he arrived and fast answers how he had driven).

Conjunctions

These are very useful little words, such as: and, but, next, then. They are used to join two parts of a sentence together which are equally important; as their name implies they form a junction or joining of two lengthy main clauses which could form sentences of their own, but which are linked strongly in subject or sequence. The ways in which they are used are:

(a) To link two parts of a sentence which could stand as independent sentences but are connected by topic, e.g.:

The letter was short *but* it included all the important points.

(b) To link an important dependent clause to the main one, where the clause enlarges on the main sentence by giving relevant facts, e.g.:

The manager decided to telephone head office, *as* he wished to obtain their authorisation for an important decision.

(c) To link more than one adjective or adverb, e.g.:

The office was light *and* warm.

(d) To link nouns, pronouns, or verbs, e.g.:

Jones *and* Brown will attend the meeting tomorrow.
Customers come *and* go all the time.

(e) To make a contrast or give an alternative, e.g.:

We can *either* go today *or* next week.

The following are the most usual conjunctions:

and, but, or, next, then, since, so, because, though, although, after, unless

There are also some which appear with other words attached to them, e.g. as soon as, in order that.

There are also some which appear in pairs, as in (e) above.

Prepositions

These are used in two important ways:

(a) To indicate a location or position—the most common words that are used in this sense are: to, from, in, into, on; e.g.:

He walked *to* the bank every morning.
She put the report *on* the desk.

(b) To indicate a method as in by or with; e.g.:

He travelled to work *by* car.
She went *with* him to share expenses.

In other words, they show a relationship between one object, person or idea and another, and thus precede a noun or pronoun. They are also exceptionally used as part of a verb, often colloquially e.g.:

She never *gets down to* work until late.

Interjections

These are only used in direct speech, and therefore enter little into banking terminology. However, if you ever write out very full notes for a speech, you may come across some, as follows:

> I would like to welcome you all, Ladies and Gentlemen, on this important occasion.

Here the nouns 'Ladies and Gentlemen' are *interjected* into the sentence.

All these parts of speech play essential roles in the construction of sentences and paragraphs; if the parts of speech are the bricks of our language, the sentence and paragraph are the framework of the building. We now need to look at how these are formed.

SECTION C ESSENTIAL SYNTAX: PUTTING THE PARTS OF SPEECH TOGETHER; CONSTRUCTING SENTENCES AND PARAGRAPHS

Sentences

Earlier we looked at why 'referring to your letter' does not constitute a sentence and why it would have to change to 'I am referring' or 'I refer' or add a clause with a main verb to be correct. Some people can recognise automatically when a sentence is complete—usually those that have had the fundamental structures taught to them at such a young age and are so thoroughly drilled that it *appears* automatic, like any skill at which one is expert. Many, however, find this difficult, so we will give the rules here.

What is a sentence? The easiest definition is that it is a group of words complete in itself which conveys an independent meaning; however, this is really too vague.

Much more specifically, a sentence is the most fundamental unit; it always begins with a capital letter and usually ends with a full stop (it can occasionally end in a question mark or exclamation mark instead); it *must* contain certain elements:

(1) a subject (except in the case of a direct command or certain idiomatic phrases where it is implied or understood);

(2) a complete (or finite) verb (a participle is not enough—see page 230, 'the dangling participle');

(3) the remainder of the sentence, which may be constructed in a variety of ways.

(2) and (3) together are known as the *predicate*.

Let's look at these in slightly more detail:

The Subject This is almost always a noun or a pronoun, e.g.:

The *clerk* wrote the letter.
She wrote the letter.
What was written?

There are, however, two exceptions where the subject is unstated but understood:

(a) in a direct command, e.g.:

Don't (you) send that letter!

(b) in common expressions which have become accepted, e.g.:

(I) thank you for your letter.

The Verb and the Rest of the Predicate We have already defined verbs. Sentences contain finite verbs which have three elements:

(a) They are either singular or plural: (I) am or (We) are.

(b) They are written in a 'person':

I (first person)
You (second person)
He/she/it (third person)

(c) They are written in a 'tense' (present, past or future), e.g.:

I write/you wrote/he will write

They also fall into two distinct groups which govern the construction of the rest of the sentence, or predicate. These are:

(a) *Transitive verbs*—these describe an action carried out to an *object* (here meaning a thing or a person). This object can be a noun, a pronoun or even a clause, e.g.:

subject	*verb*	*object*
The customer	signed	the cheque, (noun)
The customer	signed	it, (pronoun)
The customer	signed	what appeared to be a cheque, (clause)

(b) *Intransitive verbs*—these verbs, usually those describing a state of being or feeling, often take a *complement*. This means something which *completes* the subject—which gives you more information about the subject or is even interchangeable with it, e.g.:

subject	*verb*	*complement*
John	is	a clerk, (here John and the clerk are the same thing)
John	is	efficient, (here efficient tells you the essential quality about John)

Occasionally, intransitive verbs too can take a clause or phrase rather than one word to complete their meaning, e.g.:

Eight o'clock is *too late to arrive.*

Predicates in general, then, are made up of the verb, and an object or complement. They may also contain any number of phrases or clauses; sometimes these may play a major part in the sentence, as we have seen. It may be useful to give some brief definitions of clauses and phrases here.

Clauses and Phrases

(a) Clause: a clause is a group of words which form a major component of a sentence; it therefore has a subject and a finite verb of its own. It is joined to the sentence itself by a conjunction. There are two types of clauses:

(i) One which really stands as a sentence on its own but is linked to the other part of the sentence strongly; it is therefore known as a main clause, e.g.:

She is an excellent employee and *she always submits accurate work.*

(ii) One which depends on the main sentence, but gives important further information or conditions. This is known as a dependent clause, e.g.:

He finished the report, *although he had to stay behind for an hour to do so.*

(b) Phrase: a phrase is a much shorter group of words which form a small part of the sentence; phrases do not have a finite verb and are usually introduced by either prepositions or participles, e.g.:

In the report, he stated his recommendations clearly.
Referring to your letter of 10 May 19. ., I have now checked your standing order.

In this last example, where the phrase is introduced by a participle, it must be dependent on the main sentence. See again page 230.

Style in Sentence Structure Sentences should contain one idea or fact and can give some points which arise from that, or are dependent upon it. They should *not* contain many facts or ideas—they can become very confusing if they do. Sentences which are simple and short have the advantage that they always convey their meaning quickly and clearly. However, they do need to be balanced by longer, more complex sentences—otherwise the style becomes abrupt and rather jerky. In constructing complex sentences care must be taken to avoid confusion and keep the 'fog factor' to a minimum (see page 70) if they are to be comprehensible.

Words are the basic parts of the language which must be contained in the sentence framework to make complete sense. Sentences in their turn need to be grouped together to cover a subject or topic. These groups are known as paragraphs, and paragraphing well helps to guide the reader through the topics being discussed.

Paragraphing: Grouping Sentences Together

The paragraph is a very important method of indicating a topic or subject area within any document. Occasionally, for example in reports, a paragraph may actually be introduced by a topic subheading. In others, such as letters, the initial sentence of each paragraph often expresses the main subject which that paragraph will explore, although sometimes this major 'topic sentence', as it is sometimes known, will occur later in the paragraph. The important point is that it should be clearly identifiable by the reader—like the subheading, it is a signpost and acts as a guide.

Clear paragraphing is essential to the understanding of the reader, particularly when the document has to deal with a number of topics.

Apart from the topic sentence itself, paragraphs rarely contain more than four related points, otherwise they become difficult to follow. They can be of varying lengths, but you should usually avoid the very lengthy or very short. One exception to this is in letters, which normally have a brief introductory paragraph, where the writer refers to previous correspondence—this may contain only one sentence.

Paragraphing is, of course, usually indicated by indentation although with the blocked style it is often shown by a double line space. The important principles are that paragraph divisions should be clearly visible, and the sentences within them identifiably related to one topic.

The final aid to understanding and writing clear, comprehensible English is good punctuation and we will now turn our attention to this aspect of the written word.

SECTION D PUNCTUATION: MAKING THE POINTS

Punctuation is essential in English to ensure that what has been written is understandable and unambiguous; it denotes the beginning of new sentences and topics, indicates pauses, and shows direct speech and quotations. It also identifies abbreviations. There are some simple rules to be followed for each punctuation mark, and we will deal with each in turn.

The Full Stop

The main function is to end a sentence, but it is also used to denote abbreviations and initials, e.g.:

Mrs. K. B. Yates, B.Sc.

(NB In open punctuation, block style letters, full stops may be omitted.)

It is worth noting that the full stop often appears after two or three letters, not one, as in Mrs. or B.Sc. (Bachelor of Science). These really have to be learned, but reference lists are available in any dictionary. Some common abbreviations have Latin origins, e.g.:

etc. et cetera (meaning 'and the rest')
e.g. exempli gratia (meaning 'for example')

Some are very common in correspondence, such as Enc(s)., standing for enclosure(s).

The Question Mark and the Exclamation Mark

These, too, may end sentences, and always require a capital letter after them to start the next sentence.

(a) Question mark: it is important to recognise that they must be used after sentences which are so common that you sometimes forget that they are questions at all, e.g.:

Would you be good enough to fill in the enclosed form?
May I express my concern?

(b) Exclamation mark: you will rarely use these, as they are more suited to the novel or journalism than a banker's letter—they most often appear in direct reported speech. However, they do sometimes appear on urgent notices, e.g.:

Look out! There's a thief about!

In speech they either express a direct command as in:

Please get this done at once!

or they denote enthusiasm, astonishment, etc.

Capital Letters

The three punctuation marks we have discussed are always followed by a capital letter to begin a new sentence. Other uses in English include proper nouns (see page 228), the pronoun 'I' and titles (e.g. the Bank Manager; the Lord Chancellor) where *one* specific person is implied. There are many bank managers in the UK, for example, but within one branch, the job title will always be the Bank Manager.

The Semicolon

This is an extremely useful punctuation mark; however, many people seem unaware of its function. It can be used instead of a full stop or a conjunction—in other words, where the clauses that it links together could stand as separate sentences but are closely connected, e.g.:

> She has worked very hard this year; it is not surprising that she has been promoted.

It helps to give variety and avoids an overuse of conjunctions.

The Colon

A colon usually introduces a list, a quotation or direct speech, e.g.:

> The following committee members sent apologies for absence:
>
> L. M. Brough   P. L. Bowers
> S. L. Brown
>
> The Chairman began: 'Ladies and Gentlemen . . .'.

The Comma

Commas are often misused or overused. You should note that unlike the semicolon they *cannot* be used to substitute for a full stop or conjunction; they denote only a short pause, between individual words or to end or introduce short phrases. Specifically, they should only be used as follows:

(a) After one or two words on which the rest of a sentence depends or to introduce a letter, e.g.:

However, . . .
As a consequence, . . .
Dear Sir, . . .

(b) To separate a brief dependent clause or phrase from the main sentence, e.g.:

When he arrived, he went straight to the manager's office.

(c) To interject a further brief thought or fact into a sentence, e.g.:

The customer, who was late, went straight to the manager's office.

Note here the difference made to the meaning if the commas are omitted: The customer who was late went straight to the manager's office. The first merely indicates that this particular customer happened to be late; the second describes the customer's behaviour.

(d) To separate items in a list introduced by a colon, e.g.:

The following items were ordered: envelopes, headed notepaper, pencils and pens.

(e) To separate a list of adjectives, e.g.:

The letter was confused, badly written, illegible and full of errors.

A comma is *not* needed where there is a conjunction such as 'and' or 'but'.

The Apostrophe

This probably causes more confusion than any other punctuation mark; it is a characteristic of the English language in particular, and follows clearly defined rules. It is used in the following ways:

(a) In abbreviations: the apostrophe is used to show where a letter or a number of letters are omitted, e.g.:

This can't (cannot) be right; you'd (you had) better 'phone (telephone) to check.

NB This is also the one occasion when 'it's' has an apostrophe—when it abbreviates 'it is', e.g.:

It's a good report.

(b) To show possession: where 'of' has been omitted.

NB This *only* applies to nouns; pronouns *never* take an apostrophe.

The position of the apostrophe varies in regular and irregular nouns and in the singular/plural. The rules are as follows:

(i) *Regular nouns*, which make their plurals by adding 's':

Singular: apostrophe appears *before* the 's', e.g.:

The clerk's desk (the desk of one clerk)

Plural: apostrophe appears *after* the 's', e.g.:

The clerks' desks (the desks of many clerks)

(ii) Nouns ending in 'y' in the singular and 'ies' in the plural (see page 218):

Singular: apostrophe appears after the 'y' and before the 's', e.g.:

The company's accounts (the accounts of the company)

Plural: apostrophe appears after the 'ies', e.g.:

The companies' accounts (the accounts of many companies)

The above example is frequently confused, so be on your guard.

(iii) *Irregular nouns*: some irregular nouns, as we have seen, make their plurals in unique ways by changing their form. When this occurs, the apostrophe always *precedes* the 's' whether in the singular or plural, e.g.:

A man's raincoat
Men's raincoats
The memorandum's purpose
the memoranda's purposes

(c) In phrases of time or place to replace 'of', e.g.:

One month's salary
Several months' salary
The journey's end

(d) In some words which are proper names already ending in 's' and where 'of' has been omitted, an apostrophe and a further 's' is added, e.g.:

St. James's Square (the square of St. James)

The Dash and Brackets

The dash and/or brackets are used in very similar ways—to insert a further fact or idea into a sentence, e.g.:

> This report used a questionnaire as a method of investigation (see Appendix 1).
> The bank book—like everything else he carried—was immaculate.

The dash, however, can also be used singly, e.g.:

> His report was excellent—though rather brief.

The Hyphen

The hyphen acts as a link between two parts of a word in the following cases:

(a) When two parts of a word need to be pronounced separately, usually where there is a prefix, e.g.:

> co-opt, re-elect

(b) When a word cannot fit on to a line—although the dash must come in a sensible, understandable place, i.e. after one or two whole syllables. When in doubt about hyphens, consult a dictionary.

Inverted Commas and Quotation Marks

Inverted commas are used:

(a) To show direct speech; they appear *only* round the words spoken, e.g.:

> 'Well, Mr Brown,' said the manager, 'I think we can manage this loan for you.'

(b) To show quotations or titles of books, films, etc. (but not people), e.g.:

> I am going to see 'Hamlet'; in the play there is a famous speech beginning, 'To be or not to be, that is the question'.

NB When quotations or titles come in the same sentence a contrast between single and double inverted commas is used, e.g.:

> 'I am going to see "Hamlet" tonight', she said.

(c) For the names of ships, e.g. the SS 'Canberra'.

Punctuation in English is actually more logical than its spelling, so we hope that reference to these rules will help you to punctuate accurately.

Following all the principles included in the supplement should help you to communicate correctly in all the documents which you produce—and therefore to communicate effectively.

Index